Shirley Adams'
Belt Bazaar

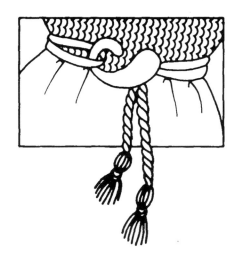

Other Books Available From Chilton
Robbie Fanning, Series Editor

Shirley Adams' Belt Bazaar

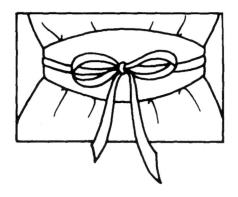

Chilton Book Company
Radnor, Pennsylvania

Published in Radnor, Pennsylvania 19089,
by Chilton Book Company

Designed by Martha Vercoutere

Edited by Robbie Fanning, Rosalie Cooke,
and Gaye Kriegel

Produced by Meredith Phillips and Robbie
Fanning

Cover and interior photographs by Mark
Jenkins

Illustrations by Deva

Manufactured in the United States of
America

Library of Congress Cataloging in
Publication Data

Adams, Shirley, 1933-

    [Belt Bazaar]
    Shirley Adams' belt bazaar

    p. cm.—(Star Wear)
    Includes index.
    ISBN 0-8019-8528-5

    1. Belts (Clothing) 2. Belt buckles.
3. Textile crafts. I. Title. II. Series.

TT668.A33 1995   94-33446
646.4'8—dc20   CIP

1 2 3 4 5 6 7 8 9 0   4 3 2 1 9 8 7 6 5

Contents

Foreword by Robbie Fanning

Shirley Adams' *Sewing Connection* TV show has many fans, myself included. We love her creative use of fabric and her encouraging approach: "You can do it!" she says in many ways.

I once attended a Shirley Adams presentation at a fabric store. She had brought over 50 garments and dazzled us with clever ideas. I scribbled and sketched madly in my notebook, along with the rest of the overflowing audience. But my favorite moment was when she said, "Feel free to come up and examine my garments. And you will find mistakes." She told us a story about making a Perfectly Tailored Suit in college. She ripped and resewed until it was perfect enough for a rare A— then gave the garment away. It was no fun to sew.

A lot of us consider our waists an imperfect part of our imperfect bodies. We try to hide our waists under large shirts, sweaters, or caftans. We may think that belts are not a part of our sewing lives.

I know Shirley would say "Nonsense!" In this book, she shows again and again how to flatter an outfit by echoing shapes, textures, or colors in a belt. It becomes a mini-palette that allows you to practice many techniques and use up fabric scraps. The time invested is minimal, yet the outcome is priceless.

Shirley tells you to assess your flamboyance factor, then make belts to fit your lifestyle. From the simplest quick belt to the most elaborate fleece-core belt, the ideas in this little gem of a book will keep you happily sewing, imperfectly or not, for the rest of your life.

Preface

From time to time, I've shown belts in live seminars or in television presentations. That sampling brought a deluge of requests for more. The result is this entire book devoted to inspiring ideas for belts you can design and the how-to instructions for making them.

I urge you not to stop with what is explained here. Rather, accept this as a starter from which you can develop some completely original creations of your own.

Enjoy!

Commercial Trims

Let your fabric speak. It won't say the same thing to every listener, and that is why an infinite variety is possible within any of the design ideas offered here. Begin with an interesting fabric and a belt almost makes itself. The more elaborate the fabric, the more simple the treatment should be; the more plain the fabric, the more it asks you to add designs to it. Have fun with the linings too, making them as appealing as the exterior.

The fabric I chose here suggested simple embellishments, like using commercial trims. Any fabric, thick or thin, woven or knit, can be used as a base. When fused to the fleece core, any fabric becomes firm enough to support commercial trims.

(top) One yard of a gold soutache braid accents the basic fabric, a heavy peacock-blue and gold brocade. I pinned and stitched ever-increasing lengths of trim in a sunburst design, tucking its ends between layers before machine stitching together. Then I pinned a costume jewelry gold pin at the sunburst base.

(middle) Black velvet with a gold harlequin pattern formed the base of this belt. I then hand-stitched a purchased appliqué to the finished belt. Quick and easy, this approach is simply a matter of finding a fabric and an embellishment that are compatible.

(bottom) To complement the metallic copper and black zebra-striped lamé, I cut 1/2 yard of a copper sequined braid into three strips, each 6" long. I sewed them by hand to the outside layer, folding ends to the backside before stitching the outside to the lining layer. I completed the belt by machine except in the sequined area, where I joined the edges by hand. A simple lining finished the backside.

Buckles

Introduction

One day I wore one of my twisted cord belts while shopping in the most exclusive shops in a large city. I made it from 15 – 20 strands of linen yarn, silk cord, and synthetic suede. The ends were attached to a nice two-piece buckle that I'd found in a fabric store.

As usual, I didn't plan to buy anything in these shops full of expensive items. Instead, I shopped for good ideas that could be simulated in the sewing room.

To my surprise, everywhere I went someone asked, "Could you please tell me where you bought that belt?" With everything around me costing thousands of dollars, do you think I would admit this belt was made out of odds and ends from my sewing room? No way! Instead I replied, "I'm sorry, but it's one-of-a-kind. It was designed for me."

Actually, that statement is true of everything you make. It *is* designed just for you!

A belt is a wonderful bridge to unite a top and bottom, set the mood as dressy or casual, turn a daytime dress into a festive evening gown, or add the panache a finished look demands.

Belts are simple to make, take almost no time, and act as mini-samplers, allowing you to play with color, texture, and technique on a small scale.

I have literally hundreds of belts because they're such fun and so easy to make. Designing and making belts becomes addictive as you look around and everything you see triggers a belt idea.

Perhaps a belt was once cinched at the waist to prevent the loss of a skirt or pair of pants. Have you ever known that tragedy to befall a woman? Nor I, as larger hips prevent that embarrassment in most cases.

We may as well admit that a belt has more than a utilitarian function, and that *visual appeal* is actually its reason for existence.

The belt unifies an outfit, pulls it together, provides a finished look. It lends a clue to the dressing theme with a soft femininity or a no-nonsense business air. It gently hints at a waistline or shouts Hey-here-I-am-look-at-me! Sportily casual or elegantly dressy, a varied collection of belts can make a chameleon of one simple dress. A belt is indeed a fashion accessory, and the spice that piques interest.

Classic clothes seem fresh year after year with different belts to update them as fashions change. The same dress can go to work by day, and to a party at night, with a switch of belts to transform it. A belt sets the mood much the same as does jewelry. If wearing an outfit the same way every time bores you, think how several alternative belts can inject a shot of fashion adrenaline.

The optical illusions a belt creates are pure magic if better proportions result from lengthening the legs, shortening the upper body, defining the waistline under an ample bust. Whatever the personal figure concern, thoughtful consideration of a belt's contribution will aid in a solution. I will comment on these proportions as we investigate four types of belts in this book:

Soft Belts—single and double layer
Stiff Belts—straight and contoured
Fleece-Core Belts—contoured and obi
Corded Belts—suede, yarns, cords, woven
    fabrics

I'll also show you some of my belts on Design Pages throughout the book, explaining what I was thinking as I made the belts.

Let's get started by exploring ideas and collecting supplies.

Finding Ideas, Collecting Supplies

Ideas

Belts out in the marketplace are absolutely fantastic. The variety of styles, sizes, materials used, textural interests, as well as price, covers an enormous range. There is indeed something available for everyone and it's yours for the buying—or better, borrow ideas and make your own!

Start out by shopping designer departments and boutiques. Their displays will show garments accessorized with belts to provide the finishing touch.

Don't neglect the fashion magazines, catalogs, pattern books, and newspapers that picture women in fashionable clothes. Yours for the clipping and collecting are a myriad of ideas you may copy or adapt. Movies, television, women you encounter in everyday living—all surround, envelop us in marvelous ideas if we will only observe. File away that idea in a little niche of the mind, or better yet, on paper for positive recall.

The belts I love, kept in glass cases (warning sign of "this is expensive") might cost several hundred dollars. Can you honestly justify such an expenditure considering how long you will wear it, fickle as fashion is? This is one of the reasons it makes good sense to create your own.

Supplies

Armed with all those ideas, search through your sewing room, the kitchen catch-all drawer, the garage workbench, or any other unlikely location where interesting objects that could become parts of belts might hide. Collect all these treasures in one box or drawer—your rich resource upon which to draw when the creative urge calls you to action.

Keep adding to this resource drawer year after year. In a hardware store, you don't know what it is, but that metal object is interesting. Vacationing on the beach may turn up a lovely shell into which nature has already perforated a couple of holes. A walk in the woods may uncover an interestingly odd-shaped small piece of wood. The possibilities are endless, and a searching eye will ferret out objects most wouldn't rate a second glance. Finding artistic uses for strange bits and pieces is not only the mark of a creative person, but probably also the mark of the inhabitant of a cluttered house. Some of us are incurable, but the addiction is justifiable if eventually we put these collections to good uses. When you realize how easily objects found around the home can be used to improvise needed parts, continue on this note and create all manner of marvels.

Shops to Haunt

Then, too, you can shop for what you need at a variety of stores.

- Fabric shop notions department
- Leather shop for leather, suedes, etc.
- Craft shop for endless treasures
- Yarn shop for interesting textural effects
- Ready-to-wear accessories department for the separate buckles they sometimes sell
- Gift shops in vacation areas for ideas as well as supplies

Belt Supplies

Collect any of the following to create belts:

- Strips of faux suede or leather
- Real suede, leather or other non-endangered skins
- Fabrics from velvets to satins, wools, cottons, anything woven or knit
- Ribbons
- Cords as filler
- Cords for decorative applications
- Cords as the actual belt
- Beads, baubles, stones, studs, shells, coins, feathers, fur, or any decorative object you think a belt needs
- Variety of buckles, rings, fasteners, hooks and eyes, Velcro® strips

When you've collected treasures until your cup runneth over, saved scraps until your husband threatens to contribute it all to the trash man, garnered ideas to the point that your mind is overburdened, then it is high time you get to work and produce. Make belts for your wardrobe exclamation points, and belts to give for special occasions to special people.

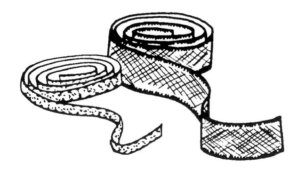

Basic Sewing Supplies and Equipment

- Sewing machine
- Iron, ironing board
- Needles, thread, pins
- Scissors, rotary cutter, craft knife
- Measuring tape
- Rulers
- Gluestick for temporary hold
- Craft glues, which will work on some materials
- Fusible web and paper-backed fusible web (heavyweight and lightweight)
- Fusible interfacing and fleece or craft felt when "beefing up" is needed
- Pattern paper—I use 1" dotted tracing paper, which I buy in a lifetime supply from a paper supply house, but any paper will do. I am less fond of the gridded interfacing-like tracing material.

Plant Influences

Simply looking around outside of your home can inspire all sorts of great ideas. Maybe it's a flower you find, or just interesting grasses, or the abstract impressions of plants. Notice how a horizontal tree branch curves gracefully. The soft lines lend themselves to clothing designs. The branch and its attached leaves can easily be duplicated in faux suede. Fuse in place, then secure with a straight stitch. If the fabric is woven or a knit, satin stitch the edge in place.

(top) I cut these windblown leaves in the colors of a challis shawl that goes with a burgundy cotton knit dress. I made the belt lining of the same knit fabric and wide enough to wrap around from the back to almost meet at the raw edges in front. I then covered these edges with a suede strip before applying the leaves in a flowing, curvy design. Notice how much narrower this belt is than many others. You determine the size.

(middle) This design was copied from a piece of jewelry. I cut acorns and oak leaves in appropriate suede colors, accented by darker stitching. Narrow straight suede strips curve easily into graceful shapes as you stitch. I made the top layer slightly smaller so the lining layer edge looks like a piping.

(bottom) These water lilies show that the tiniest scraps of suede can be useful. To avoid the necessity of stitching, attach such small pieces with the heavy-duty paper-backed fusible web. Try fabric combinations first on scraps to make sure they will work. For example, suede will not fuse to lamé so it requires stitching.

Soft Belts

(top) This composition two-piece buckle looks like a slice of agate, but it is manufactured by one of the button companies. A single layer of soft suede is stitched to each piece.

(middle) A one-piece buckle has a slot at either end through which suede or fabric can be looped. Tuck the ends to the underside when the belt is in place on your waist.

(bottom) An expensive buckle justifies the cost if it is not permanently committed to one belt. You can interchange the belt strips with each wearing.

Soft Belts

Soft belts, squashy and comfortable, are not reinforced by stiffened layers. They can be made from synthetic leathers and suedes or woven and knit fabrics. They may be of the garment fabric or any other fabric which seems appropriate. You can make light belts from a single layer or sturdier belts from a double layer of suede or fabric.

This section also describes a variety of fasteners and buckles for both weights of belt. They range from store-bought buckles to intriguing home-made closures. Then there are the embellishment ideas that draw on traditional methods made easy with fusibles and sewing machine.

No patterns are included in this section of the book as it's simply a matter of measuring your waist and adding the necessary extra for an overlap or tie. Some dimensions are suggested here and there which you can accept as given, or modify to your liking.

Quick Belts

From sporty canvas-look stretch belting to evening's stretch sequins, you can find a big selection of belting sold by the yard in fabric stores. These make the quickest belts. All that's needed is the addition of a buckle or hook. Just be sure to have with you a swatch of your dress fabric for matching the perfect belt complement.

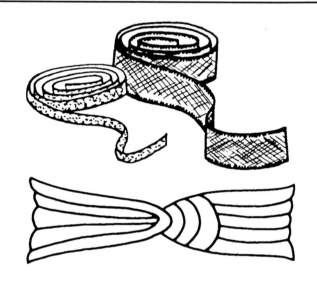

Basic Synthetic Suede Soft Belt

One of my favorite materials for a single layer belt is heavier weight synthetic suede, which simply can be cut without finishing edges. What is terrific about this material is that the crosswise direction expands and contracts—and that's wonderful for those who breathe, eat, or otherwise need some variance. It moves with you.

Not only does it flex, but also it is soft and crushy. That means it will feel fine when you sit or bend over and won't poke your ribs uncomfortably. It makes a lovely belt in a huge color range to match or complement whatever you wish.

One layer of synthetic suede is flattering and comfortable to even large waistlines. Because synthetic suede is sold in 45" widths, the maximum waistline measurement for one width is 38". (A single knot needs 7".) If your waist is larger than that, you will need to piece the length of the belt. You can knot it and have a speck at the ends to tuck inside the belt to keep it neat. If your waist is smaller than 38", or you make the belt longer, the ends will hang down gracefully when knotted—leave it casual.

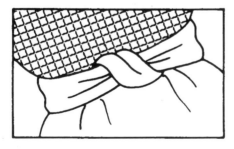

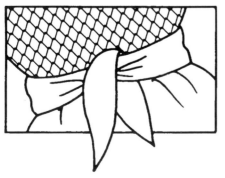

1. Use a strip of scrap suede left over from a sewing project or go to the fabric shop and buy it by the inch. A 4"-wide strip is a good size. Piece strips if necessary.

- Cutting that belt strip wider so it crushes still more, and shorter so it ties in a perky single knot can also be attractive.

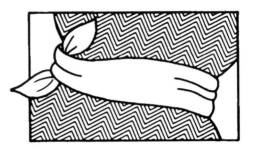

2. Keep the ends cut off straight as from the bolt, or modify them with new cuts in whatever shape pleases you.

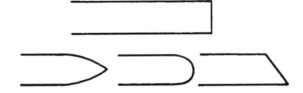

3. See page 18 for embellishment ideas and page 10 for possible fasteners.

How to Line a Suede Belt

This single thickness of suede may seem too flimsy to add embellishment. The belt appears more finished and more luxurious if you apply lining fabric to the backside.

1. Cut the lining fabric to the same size and shape as the belt, but with added seam allowances.

2. Press under the fabric raw edges.

3. With wrong sides together, edgestitch lining to suede belt. You might find it more to your liking to use fabric glue to secure the pressed-under fabric edges to the backside rather than stitching.

How to Reinforce a Suede Belt

Anytime you have to cut into the single-layer suede belt, for example, to add a buckle with a prong and to punch holes at the other end, reinforce the belt (only in the area of the hole if the thin crushy quality of a single layer is desirable throughout the rest of the belt).

1. Before punching holes, cut two oval or round shapes 1/2" larger than the holes will be—one of suede and a matching one of fusible web.

2. Place fusible web shape on the backside of the belt, centering over the area of the holes. Cover web with suede shape, wrong side against web.

3. Steam press. Let cool, then punch holes through all three layers.

Soft Fabrics

There is no reason why soft fabric alone can't make a terrific single-layer belt. When you make a dress or blouse, there is always a long narrow scrap left. But to use a fabric in a single layer demands some sort of an edge finish. If this belt is of woven or knit fabric, serge the raw edges in a decorative overlock or make rolled hems all around. The exception is a fabric which does not fray and therefore already looks finished.

- If the strip is long enough, double wrap the waist.

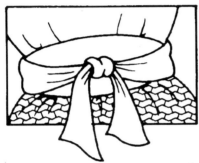

- Tie in a big floppy bow as soft fabric will nicely do.

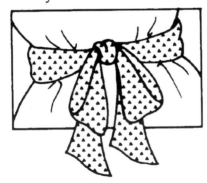

- If the fabric is crisp, a perky knot will do better—kind of a butterfly look. In fact, stitch a few bugle beads or faux jewels on the ends to emphasize that butterfly look.

- If you need a bigger impact than a narrow belt alone can give, wrap a wider, single-thickness strip of synthetic suede around your waist and wear the narrow belt on top, permitting the faux suede to show above and below. This could also act as the transition in an unusual color combination—making it appear fashionable rather than weird!

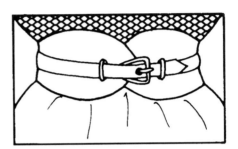

Any of the above will extend the upper body a little if the waist tie and blouse are the same fabric. Make this tie the same color as the skirt if you want to shorten the upper body.

With an overblouse, tying at the hip will look wonderful on the woman who wants to lengthen her torso (as long as she hasn't large hips).

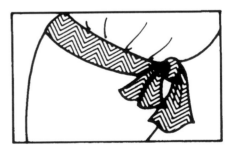

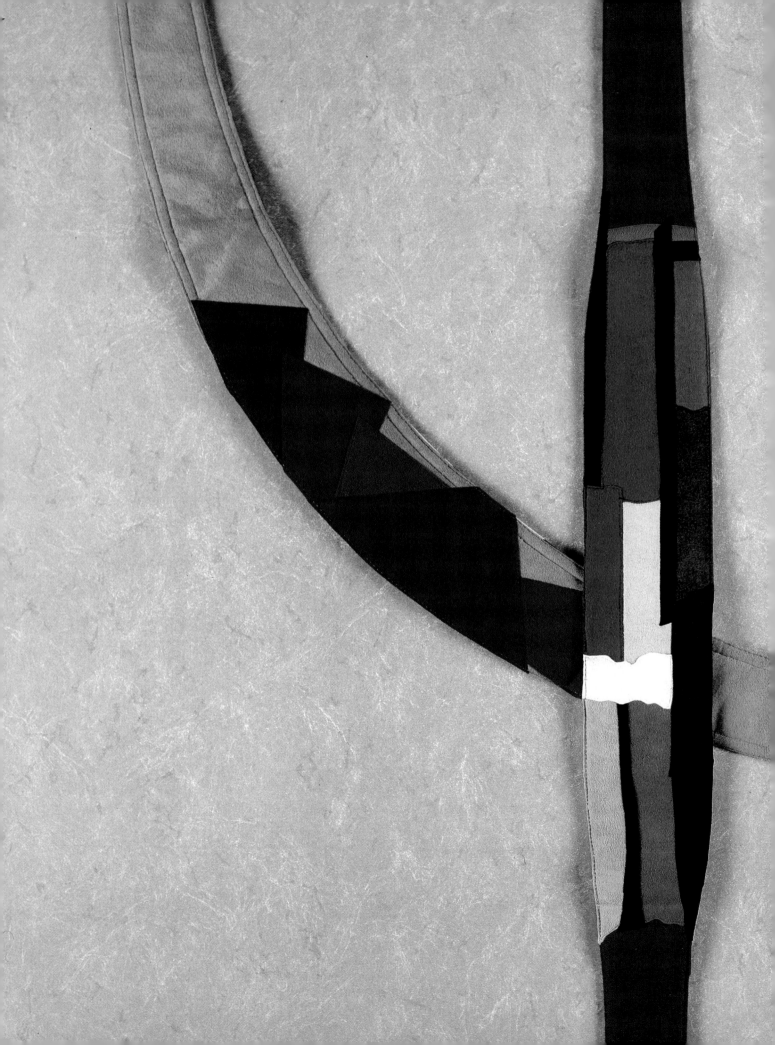

Scrap Art

(left) This color combination is borrowed from the print lining, something I do often. (If you have no color sense, borrowing the color scheme of a print is sensible.) I also often use synthetic suedes for embellishment because the raw edges do not need finishing. Here I fused wedges and triangles, then edgestitched them. A woven or knit would need to be satin-stitched to cover the raw edges.

(middle) I randomly cut pieces, inspired by the multiple colors and black outlines of the Sunday comics. This is a light-hearted treatment that would go well with summer or resort clothing right down to the cotton interlock lining.

(right) Interesting designs can happen when you play with small, irregularly shaped scraps. These were slashed in several places and fanned open, then arranged and rearranged until the composition pleased me. There is no right or wrong to this sort of designing. The only person you need to please is you. Such freedom is truly a joy.

Straight-Grain Soft Belts

Straight-grain soft belts can be made from any woven or knit fabric that is not too stiff or bulky to wrap around your waist.

1. Cut two layers of fabric from 3" to 6" wide, about 10" longer than your waist.

2. Stitch right sides together, leaving one end open and forming the other end to be angled, rounded, or pointed.

3. Turn right side out over a yardstick or wooden spoon handle. Press.

4. Secure open end around a buckle, maybe wood or plastic, or even covered with self-fabric if that won't result in an obviously home-made look. The buckle should be narrower than the belt. Because the fabric is wider and crushes through the narrower buckle, it holds in place without a prong.

Below Waist Soft Belt on Straight Grain

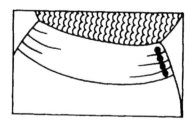

You may prefer a belt cut on the straight grain to sit below the waistline instead of above the waistline. This is especially flattering on a short-waisted person who wants to make the torso look a little longer, but not so for a woman with a long torso and short legs. Measure your waistline and also the high hip area. This high hip is only about 2" or so under the waist.

1. Cut this fabric 8" – 12" high with slightly curved edges. Make it 2" larger than waist at top edge, 2" larger than high hip at lower edge.

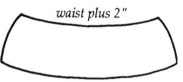

waist plus 2"

high hip plus 2"

2. Run a gathering stitch on each short end of the belt. Stitch a rolled hem top and bottom.

3. Gather ends to about 4" and bind with a small piece (5" x 7") of the same fabric, stitching right sides together.

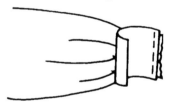

4. With right sides together, fold extension in half. Stitch two short ends. Turn, press, slipstitch opening on the backside. Turn the extension on the top layer of belt to the inside and slipstitch. The opening for these belts can be front, back, side, or wherever it looks best.

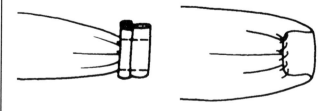

Stretchy Soft Belts

A stretchy, soft belt is comfortable to wear because of the leeway provided to sit or breathe. This will happen if you cut knit fabric on the crosswise grain, woven fabric on the bias. Thin soft fabrics work better than stiff or bulky ones.

1. Cut the fabric on the bias slightly longer than your waist measurement. Cut either single or double height, depending on the amount of fabric you have and how thin it is.

2. If cut single height, hem upper and lower raw edges with a machine-rolled hem or serge edges. If cut double height,

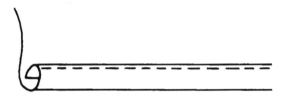

fold right sides together and stitch along the long edge. Turn right side out and press.

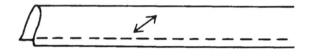

3. Gather ends and bind with a small piece (3" x 5") of the same fabric, stitching right sides together. See page 8.

4. Turn in seam allowance on opposite end of extension. With right sides together, fold extension in half. Stitch top and bottom end. Turn, press, slipstitch opening on the backside. See page 8.

5. You may completely turn under this extension and whip it to the backside, none of it extending on the outside or beyond the gathered end. See page 8.

6. Secure the belt end to the belt with Velcro®, buttons and buttonholes, or hooks and eyes, as you prefer. The opening for these belts can be front, back, side, or wherever it looks best.

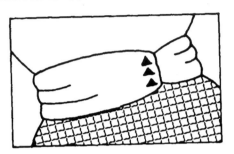

Below Waist Soft Belt on the Bias

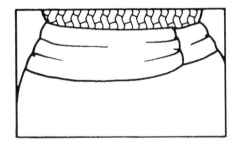

Stretchy belts are meant to be worn at the waist, upper edge going into the rib cage. If you would like to wear the belt from the waist downward, make it slightly larger to fit that high hip area.

Fasteners for Soft Belts

Store-Bought Fasteners

Search through your belt collection accumulated over the years and you may find several detachable buckles whose present belts unsnap, unlatch, or otherwise detach themselves from that buckle. You may reassign the buckle's duty among other belting strips.

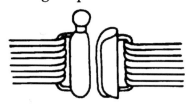

Find other interesting attachments in fabric shops, or in department store or specialty shop accessory and belt areas. Available is a whole line of flat metallic objects through which belt strips can be laced or whose ends can be tied to attach in whatever manner pleases you. Buckles, or the variety of objects that can serve that purpose, are endless—use whatever best does the job.

Depending on where you find buckles, their prices vary from a few to a bunch of dollars, but the fact that one buckle may be used repeatedly for many belts makes the investment seem worthwhile.

One-Piece Buckles

Although I mostly discuss using suede here, one-piece buckles are also suitable for wovens and knits, as long as the fabric has texture or body. Slip one end through the buckle and tack it by hand underneath. Soft or slippery fabrics will not stay in place unless you also add Velcro® or some other fastener under the belt end.

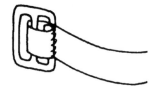

Preferably, use a one-piece buckle without a prong as strain in a concentrated area will rip the single thickness of suede. If your buckle has a prong and will never be used with belting that requires one, permanently remove the prong with a pair of pliers by bending that metal piece until it breaks off.

Because of suede's rough texture, one end can be folded over the middle brace and tucked back underneath against the body. The loose other end can be tucked

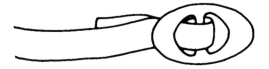

through the buckle and the texture will hold it all firmly in place without any fasteners. If this belt strip is wider than the

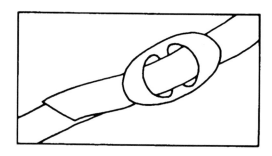

buckle, no problem, as it crushes nicely into the narrower buckle and holds even more securely because of the additional bulk.

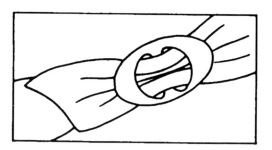

One-Piece Buckles With a Prong

When the intended buckle has a prong, whether movable or stationary, you need more than the single-layer suede.

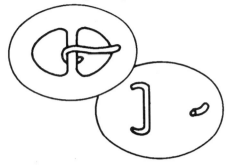

You need to provide reinforcement at the punched hole that will strain with the prong's pull. Fuse a reinforcement layer as described earlier. See page 4.

Suede Crushed into Holder

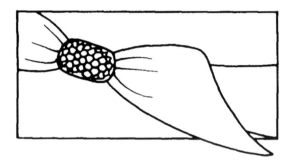

Still another variation is to cut suede about 8" longer than waist size, taper the end, and crush it into a holder. This holder can be metal (maybe a scarf clasp or a jeweled pin) or maybe the same suede or reptile skin wrapped and glued on the backside. Secure on the body by attaching Velcro® between the layers.

Two-Piece Buckles

Two-piece buckles come in many designs, narrow or wide, to flatter large or small waistlines.

On the backside of most of these buckle sections are double brackets. Weave single thickness suede or thicker leather-like belting strips through those brackets to temporarily secure and wear. These strips come in a vast array of colors and in various widths appropriate for buckle sizes.

Buckle With Hook

Another type of buckle which may be purchased packaged in fabric shops is one with a hook on the back. It includes a separate eye attachment.

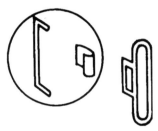

It may be used the same way as previously illustrated buckles, with belt strips temporarily tucked through and not permanently attached. I permanently attached

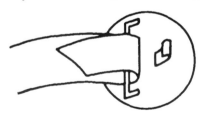

mine to a wide belt strip (5" wide). This is a thin faux suede rather than the original heavier suede, so it is soft and crushy.

1. Cut that strip the length of your waist plus 10".

2. Cut both ends in a rounded shape.

3. Crush one end through the buckle attachment and stitch it in place by hand. It can therefore be removed very easily should you decide to use the buckle on another belt.

4. Sew the eye attachment on at the spot where wrapping the belt around the waist will make it snug when fastened.

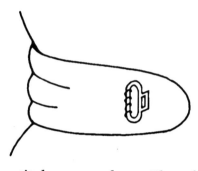

5. Your stitches may show. Therefore, if this buckle and its eye will become a permanent part of the belt because you have no plans to transfer it to another belt, it might look more professional to fold a piece of suede through the holder slot and machine stitch permanently in place.

6. To wear this, wrap the eye end snugly around the body with the eye at your center front. Then pull the buckle end around and fasten. This makes a dramatic statement focusing attention on your waistline. Supposedly such a wide belt would make you look larger—but I find

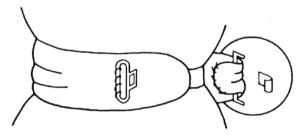

the reverse to be true. It actually makes my waistline look a little smaller than it really is. A petite person couldn't get away with this as easily as a taller person, however, as there wouldn't be enough midriff space. You have to try this in front of a mirror to see how it looks on you.

Ring Fasteners

Rings are especially appropriate for quick belts. See page 2. Remember also the round rings or D-shaped rings that come in packages of two and are a silvery or brass metal. These always have a split on the part the belt will cover. That split can be slightly pried apart to insert a fabric tubing over it if the metal would look better concealed.

Another fastener might be a bracelet with each

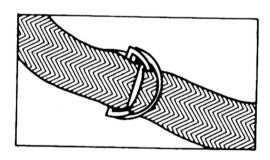

end of the belt strip tucked through it, then folded to the underside. Suede texture will hold the ring in place (not so with most other fabrics).

Covered Rings

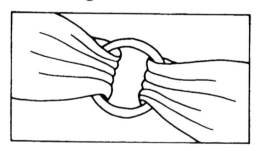

Consider winding round or D-rings with suede.

1. Cut a long strip of suede about 1/2" wide.

2. Use a little glue to permanently attach beginning and end.

3. Tightly spiral-wrap the ring.

These work nicely as buckles on which to attach all type of beltings. Knot the belt as shown. Follow with your finger or your eye closely on this twist to figure out how it works. To close, pull it into a tighter knot.

Note: This type of belt takes several more inches than a standard belt. To determine the length needed, tie a tape measure around your waist as you would a belt. Now you can see exactly how long to cut the belting.

Ring Fastener for a Short Belt

One ring can be used with a shorter belt length in the following manner:

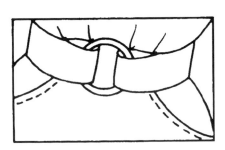

1. Cut the belting about 5" longer than your waist.

2. Stitch one side to the ring.

3. Secure the other side with sets of Velcro® dots or strips. If you want no stitching to show use Velcro® on both sides.

Home-made Fasteners for Soft Belts

Please consider the following ideas as beginnings. Change shapes in any way you consider an improvement. You will think of several more variations of these ideas.

The biggest shortcoming of most of these fastenings is lack of adjustability. If your waistline constantly fluctuates, these are not for you. Consider instead the countless suggestions in the book that do adjust.

Wedge Closure

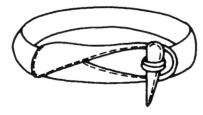

Sew a suede loop to one end and wedge closure to the other end.

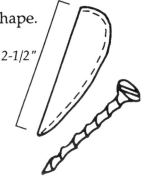

1. The wedge is a suede scrap about 2-1/2" long folded over something stiff like a long metal screw or a piece of wood or plastic.

Edgestitch around the shape.

2-1/2"

Wrap one end of the fabric belt around the wedge and stitch in place—or insert the belt inside the suede wrap before edgestitching. You can use a toggle button instead of the wedge.

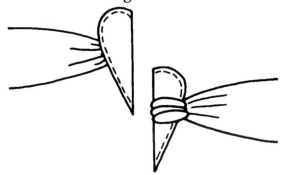

2. For the loop, cut a dog-bone shape of suede about 7" long and 1" wide at center, 2-1/2" wide at ends. A short loop, about 5" long, would also work well. Fold in half

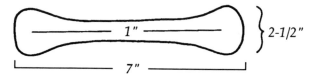

lengthwise and edgestitch only the straight center, leaving the curved ends unstitched until later.

3. With a pair of wire cutters or pliers, cut off a 6-1/2" length of wire coat hanger. Insert inside the suede bone and fold bone in half. To get the two sides even, I marked the center with a pin and bent the bone over my sewing machine cabinet door.

4. Insert the other end of the gathered fabric between layers of suede loop ends and machine stitch it all together.

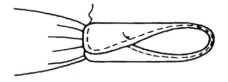

If so much stiffness sounds uncomfortable, substitute a fat rope of upholstery welting or a reasonable facsimile in place of the wire inside the loop. Place rope on the flat suede bone shape before it is stitched, and use a gluestick to temporarily hold it in place. To stitch close to that fat ridge requires a zipper or cording foot. Stitching this is easier if you cut the bone shape a little wider than you really want it. Glue, stitch, and then trim off the excess width.

Tab Closure

Use the same wedge idea on one end.

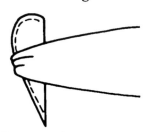

For the other suede end, cut two of this tab shape.

1. To determine the right size for the ends, make a paper pattern first and re-cut it if necessary until the size and shape work out just right.

2. Put one on the bottom, one turned over on top. Place end of fabric between layers, and stitch as shown.

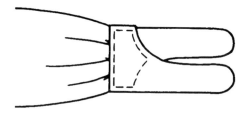

3. Fold both tabs back on top and stitch around ends, forming loops. Slip loops over top and bottom of wedge.

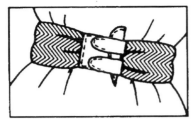

Short Tab Closure

1. Cut four of this tab end from synthetic suede pieces. This shape is similar to the one described above, but with shorter tab lengths.

2. Pair the pieces wrong sides together to make two tab ends, noting that the two suede pieces have been reversed.

3. Insert the gathered fabric end of the belt between two of the square ends and stitch all around the suede shapes. Repeat for the other end.

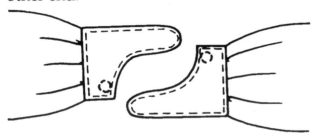

4. Attach Velcro® dots or strips to topsides of each square end and undersides of rounded tabs. The finished belt nicely meshes in place.

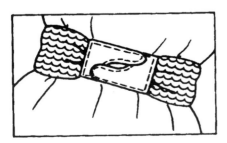

Suede Slot

Here's another variation for those end pieces.

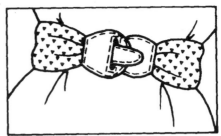

1. Cut two each of these two suede shapes. Again, play with paper until the sizes and shapes work out right.

2. Wrong sides together, stitch a slot shape on the end of B. With a craft knife, cut out the center of stitched area.

3. Cut a length of clothes hanger wire to position *between* layers as in the picture. (Use glue-stick to hold temporarily). On blunt end, insert fabric between layers and pin. Stitch all around.

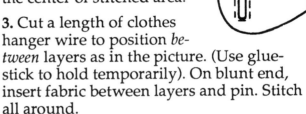

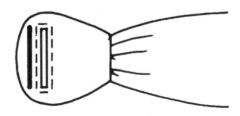

4. Insert other end of fabric between remaining two suede pieces. Stitch layers together. Apply Velcro® dot or strip as pictured. The pointed end will go through the slot from underneath and fold forward against itself to hold at the waist.

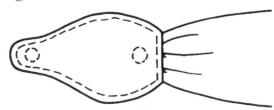

Suede Buckle

1. To reinforce the opening in this suede buckle, use a large brass ring about 2" or 3" in diameter.

2. Flatten it somewhat in a workbench vise so it becomes an oval. Better yet, what can you unearth around the house of a similar shape, but flat so the raised bulk won't be a presser foot problem?

3. Place the oval on a single suede layer, folding over the other half, so it's enclosed.

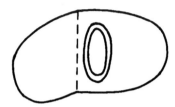

4. Stitch around the inside of the oval to hold everything secure. To accomplish this I had to remove the presser foot, remembering to lower the presser bar lever to stitch. Using something flat for the oval would be better. The foot could then remain on.

5. Using a zipper or piping foot so you can stitch close to the bulk, stitch around the outside of the oval. Cut away the inner suede close to stitching line like the hole in a doughnut.

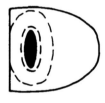

6. Insert a belt of the same or contrasting colored suede between the two layers of suede and pin or glue to hold temporarily.

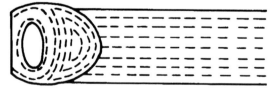

7. Add more stitching to both decorate and secure the belt to the buckle.

8. Stitch hook and eye to other belt end and under buckle to hold in place on waist. A

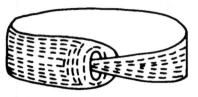

Velcro® strip can replace the hook and eye if you prefer. If your suede is big enough, make the belt and buckle all in one piece.

Loop Fasteners

Flat Loop

Instead of using rings, you can attach beltings to loops. Add a flat loop made of the belt material to one end of a belt. Stitch or glue this loop in place on the belt end.

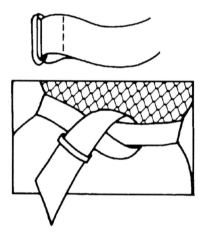

Wire-covered Loop

Cover wire to make two loops, one shorter than the other, about 3" long total.

1. Cut two strips of synthetic suede 5/8" x 5" and 5/8" x 6".

2. Fold in half lengthwise and edgestitch.

3. With a pair of wire cutters or pliers, cut off a 5" and 6" length of wire coat hanger.

4. Insert wires inside the suede.

5. Bend wires in half. To get the two sides even, I mark the center with a pin and bend the strip over my sewing machine cabinet door.

6. Twist the suede around the wire so the stitching is underneath against the body.

7. Glue all ends together and stitch or glue to belt end.

8. Wrap and glue another strip around this joining to neatly finish it off.

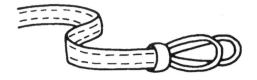

This is a good way to produce a narrow belt. Cut it longer if you want the end hanging down for a more vertical look.

Embellishing Soft Belts

These marvelous belts can be embellished in a variety of ways. Even though we get quite elaborate, the belt can blend right into your clothing and not increase the waistline's apparent size if hues, values, and intensities of colors are all kept about the same, and in the subdued rather than bright range.

Cutwork

Stitch a cutwork pattern, as is often done on linen fabrics, for a nice accent. Satin stitch this pattern on woven fabric to prevent ravelling. That also works fine on suede, but use a straight stitch to outline the pattern since ravelling is not a problem. Then use little scissors or a craft knife to cut out the little blank spaces in between leaves, flowers, or whatever design you have created.

Slash and Tie

Another thought is to cut the belt a little smaller than your waist, then with a craft knife cut slits all along the belt strip. Instead of slits, make these buttonholes if fabric ravels. Weave some cording, leather strips, or whatever you find appropriate, throughout these slashes and tie the ends in front or in back.

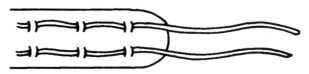

Double-Needle Stitching

Double-needle stitching produces raised pintucks on the suede strip in any pattern your imagination creates. You may need to

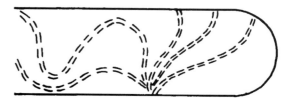

tighten upper tension to produce raised pintucks. Experiment with the different widths of needle to see what you like best. Rather than buy two spools of thread, you can always wind off thread onto a bobbin and use it as the second spool. On some machines you will treat both threads as one through the tension disks; on others, you will separate the threads. Consult your machine manual or sewing machine dealer.

For an evening look, use metallic threads.

Appliqué

Embellish a strip with a collage of interestingly colored or textured fabric strips appliquéd on the surface. Find a leather

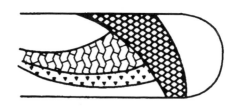

shop and purchase scraps or a whole skin of beautifully colored and textured snake or lizard to appliqué to the suede strip. Feathers, beads, stones, yarns, and cords can embellish it. Unleash that creative imagination and come up with designs so fascinating that they beg for duplication to give as gifts to lucky friends and family.

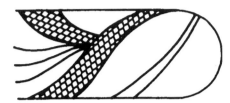

- You may want to use a gluestick to temporarily hold appliquéd layers in place before machine stitching.

- If the appliqués are of woven fabrics, satin stitch in place to completely cover and prevent raveling raw edges.

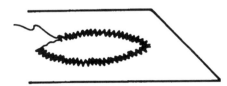

- Use bias-cut strips of other fabrics with their edges folded under to stitch over raw edges, offering yet another pattern or texture.

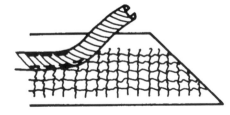

- If not concerned with raveling (as with suede or skins), edgestitch with a straight stitch.

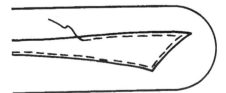

Store-Bought Appliqués

Look also in the fabric shop for appliqués already made of sequins, seed pearls, and bugle beads in imaginative shapes and designs like paisley, flower shapes, and diamonds. You can attach them to a satin or other dressy belt.

Reptile Appliqué

Reptile, a real skin or a fake, produces an interesting contrast when appliquéd on a piece of suede cut about 10" to 12" longer than waist measurement.

1. Zigzag or straight stitch in place.

2. Because of the stiffness, it will probably be safe to punch holes. Use a buckle with a stationary prong, or even a standard buckle with a movable prong.

3. Slightly crush or pleat the end of the belt so it's narrow enough to attach to the buckle bracket.

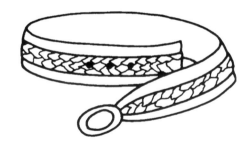

Cording

Some cording or welting has a flat tape attached which may be sewn easily in place. To conceal it, cover that tape under a strip of suede, leather, or the bias-cut strips.

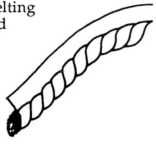

Collage

A collage of assorted origins is an interesting and absorbing endeavor. While the creative enthusiasm is still flowing, check your accumulated treasures for a silken cord to border the snake or intermingle in the overall design.

Glue those silken cords in place or couch on using a zigzag stitch in blending color thread or monofilament invisible nylon.

If you stitch on by hand, anchor stitches midway in the cord so they don't show on the surface.

- Have you some beads, small stones, or shells crying to join the melange?
- Add larger stones or shells with opportune natural holes to the belt with a few stitches. Notice on some ready-made belts that large unblemished shells, stones, wood, or metal plates are attached with fastenings of thin leather thongs, silken cords, or other encumbering sinews that accomplish the task.

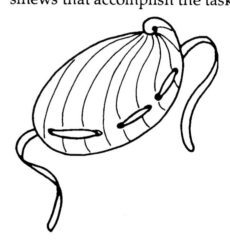

Rings as Embellishment

A succession of rings or bracelets may be used like this. In a craft shop, you can find

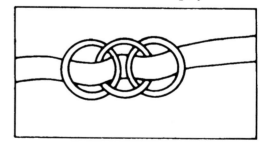

them in natural, varnished, or painted wood, plastic, metal. They can be big or small depending on your preference, your height, and the type material you will weave through them. They work equally well with soft, crushy suede or fabric, or stiffer leather or suede. Even cords or yarns are terrific.

The ends of this belt would probably be tied in back.

Synthetic Suede and Fabric

Mix fabric belts with suede scraps when there either isn't enough of one to go it alone, or just because you like the mixed effect. Here are some ideas:

- Stitch gathered front fabric edges between suede layers and tie at back.

- Stitch gathered fabric ends between suede shapes. Fasten at center by hook and eye or Velcro® snap.

Partial Cords

Braided, twisted, wrapped, or woven cords can embellish or fasten a soft belt. They may be only a 10" or 12" section in

front, stitched to fabric or suede or canvas belting which surrounds the rest of your waist. Combine whatever seems the best way either because of appearance or quantity of supplies available.

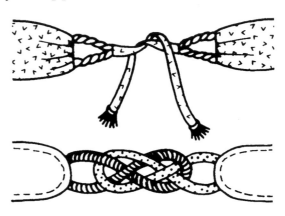

Jeweled Trim

If you make the stretchy belt for an evening dress, sew a bit of jeweled trim at the opening to lend glamour. With the popularity of faux jewels, it seems the right thing to do.

Abstract Designs

For the non-artist, abstract designs are "do-able." Begin with an idea from a plant or the buildings of a city skyline. Use a section of a car's hubcap or its front radiator grill. Simplify the design, using only a part of it. Vary or repeat the design, blow it up, or shrink it down in scale. The origin of the final product will never be recognizable, and that's just fine. It becomes interesting forms and uses the colors you want.

(vertical) I fused paper-backed fusible web to the back of multicolored synthetic suede strips. These were chosen in the same colors as the print lining fabric. I cut them in varying widths, arranged diagonally, and fused them to the belt's topside, using a heavy-duty brand of fusible that requires no stitching. (If you would prefer stitching to show, use the lighter weight fusible.) I changed thread color to match each strip. I've also made this belt with lengths of ribbon instead of suede.

(top) This simple shape is fused and stitched to the upper layer of the belt. I experimented with similar paper shapes before using the paper as a pattern to cut out the suede. Once you gain the courage and confidence to "freelance" this way rather than relying on precise directions, you'll find yourself becoming quite artistic.

(middle) These simple shapes are cut in small scraps of closely related colors to blend with an outfit. You might instead mix sharp contrasts to "legitimize" a strange color combination of skirt and blouse. The belt would pull it together for a striking whole, looking like a designer creation.

(bottom) The small design on the print wool suggested a stylized tulip of fused and stitched suede scraps. Enlarging small existing designs takes no professional capabilities. You can do it!

23

Stiff Belts

(horizontal top) I fused two shaped layers of faux suede together for extra firmness. Then I attached a two-piece buckle to the ends with other suede pieces.

(horizontal bottom) Again, I fused two layers together. In the middle I cut a window out of the top layer. Featured in its center is a perforated piece of brass attached by cords laced through.

(vertical left) The moiré taffeta both binds the edges and backs the tapestry strip before a two-piece buckle is stitched to the ends.

(vertical right) I fused double suede layers together for strength. Because the pewter buckle has a prong, I punched eyelets in the suede. Still, there will be some pulling strain.

25

Stiff Belts

Reinforced or stiffened belt layers increase still further the variety of belts you can create. Fabrics also profit from extra interior layers to "beef up" and give a more commercial quality to the belt.

Always be on the lookout for new products as they become available. Some can be useful in streamlining your sewing techniques. Others are so revolutionary you want to shout their praises to every sewer you know, and wonder why no one thought of it sooner. You find yourself saying over and over, "How did I ever live without it?"

That's what I thought years ago when the fusible webs came on the market. A slight drawback was that they had to be fused directly between two surfaces or else be protected with a Teflon press sheet. Years later, these products still have their place and at times I fall back on them.

Then the new generation of this product hit the scene, delivering what it promised and overcoming past inconvenience. This fusible web with its own peel-off protector eliminated the need for a separate Teflon sheet under the iron. Paper-backed fusible web stimulated the wearable art scene for appliquéd clothing and accessories. I use it extensively to make stiff belts.

The shapes of stiffer belts must be well thought out for appearance, but also for comfort. The soft wide belt suggested previously might be uncomfortable as a stiffer belt. Remember, it will not expand and contract because fusing the layers eliminates the stretch, as well as greatly increasing the stiffness. I don't care to sit or bend over in a belt that punches me in the ribs with every motion. Therefore, when using stiff material, I choose to make narrower belts, especially on the sides, and/or contoured belts.

When using velvet or other pile fabrics, be sure to test fusing techniques first on scraps; some velvets can be ruined, the pile mashed flat. Put a thick terry cloth towel or piece of velvet on the ironing board, pile side up. Fuse the fashion fabric with pile side down. This might preserve the look.

Shaping Stiff Belts

To contour the belt to your shape, cut it in scrap fabric or paper and try it on in front of a mirror before risking mistakes on expensive materials.

Consider the effects of various shapes:

• Contoured belts make the waist appear smaller than do straight horizontal lines. Also, the shaping means narrower sides that are more comfortable to wear and to move in.

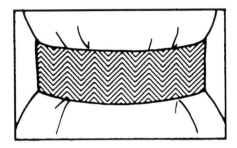

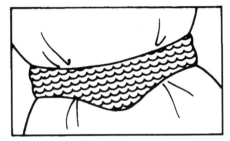

• Wearing the belt point up makes your legs appear longer and your body taller. It also decreases the size or paunch of a midriff section, but it makes the body look shorter-waisted.

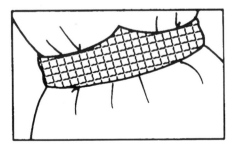

• Worn point down, this belt shortens the overall appearance while elongating the waist, shortening legs. You can't believe what a difference it makes in your appearance and the optical illusions accomplished until you try the belt both ways in front of a mirror.

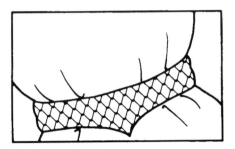

• You might try an asymmetrically contoured effect to see if this is more flattering. This off-balance treatment fools the eye and makes a waistline appear smaller than it really is.

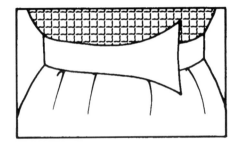

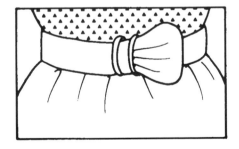

Basic Stiff Belt

Here's how to make a basic stiff belt after you've decided on your belt shape. Let's use synthetic suede and paper-backed fusible web.

1. Cut two belt layers exactly the same size.

2. Wrong sides together and with fusible web of the same size and shape sandwiched between the layers, steam press to fuse them as one. The paper-backed fusible web package will direct you about heat setting and pressing time. Be sure to protect suede with a press cloth when doing this process to avoid iron impressions and to retain the suede texture.

3. Edgestitch or topstitch to keep layers stiff and secure. See fastener ideas on page 36 and embellishment ideas on page 38.

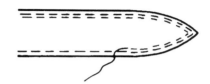

Some Stiff Belts

The Layered Belt in this section is a stiff version of a soft belt. But the Money Belt and the Purse Belt make use of the fact that belts become thicker and stronger when you add fusible web. The Fused Obi Sash and the Ribbon Belt are two highly decorative stiff belts.

Layered Belt

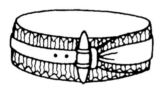

Wrap a wide, single-layer belt around your waist and wear a narrow, stiff belt on top. This idea will work with suede, fabric, or other material. Use a suede wedge fastening end. See page 13. Sometimes you can cut the fastener end and the belt all in one piece. See page 16.

Money Belt

You can use the width of a contoured belt to your advantage for another purpose. Haven't you ever traveled with more cash than you care to keep in a purse? How about making a money belt? For the contour belts, before fusing the layers together, insert a zipper in the back layer.

1. Using a craft knife, draw and cut out the space of the zipper teeth—about 7" x 1/4".

2. With a gluestick, temporarily attach the zipper to the suede underside, centering it under the opening.

3. Stitch around the edge of the zipper.

4. When fusing this belt layer to the back side of the outer belt layer, *do not* place any fusible web in the zipper area. Leave the center area clear and hollow to hold money. Then stitch around the edges in the usual way and apply end fasteners.

do not fuse here

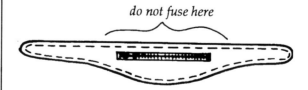

Velcro® dot stitched or glued inside flap. Its companion would be located in appropriate spot on outside of purse.

———————— Fold ————————

These slits would be longer or shorter depending on width of intended belt. For the athlete, a narrower belt's smaller slits would keep contents safer with less danger of their bouncing out. For that same person, an elasticized belt might be more comfortable.

———————— Fold ————————

This lower section will be folded up into place and the ends stitched to the center section. The other Velcro® snap is attached to the reverse side of this wherever it meshes with the one on the flap.

Purse Belt

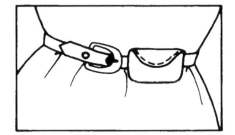

A small detachable purse attached to a stiff belt can be a fashion accessory where you put a few necessary items when you don't want to carry a large purse. It can also be just the thing for a runner, golfer, or tennis player to keep valuables safely on her person. Even if a runner wouldn't be caught dead carrying a purse, wearing this under sweats won't show!

Modify this full-size pattern to make it larger or smaller as is appropriate. A smaller size might be more to your liking if your essential contents require less space. This one is large enough to hold money or credit card, driver's license, keys. Make it a little larger and it could even hold your passport and traveler's checks.

1. Trace the pattern on another piece of paper, cut out, and fold it down in place.

2. Try it on your waist to see how the size looks. Put your necessities inside the paper trial to check for sufficient space. Then re-cut your pattern if a change of size is needed.

3. Cut the flap pointed instead of round, if you prefer.

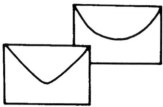

4. The fabric can be anything from denim to satin to suede. The latter or any non-ravelly fabric can be cut as is. Cut two layers and fuse together with fusible web. Or cut one suede layer and an inner layer of some other non-ravelly fabric and treat the same way. A fabric that ravels needs 1/4" seams added to all sides for finished edges. If this is a purse made entirely from fabric whose edges must be finished:

a. Cut two pieces, adding 1/4" seam allowances beyond the pattern. Interface the back of one of the two layers.

b. Right sides together, stitch the seam leaving a small opening for turning right side out. Turn, press, whip opening closed.

5. In non-ravelly fabric or suede, cut slits with a craft knife on the middle section large enough for the belt to fit through. In fabric that ravels, make machine buttonholes instead of the slits.

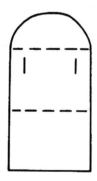

6. Edgestitch the lower edge.

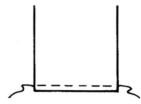

7. Fold up this lower section and stitch ends in place, continuing the stitching around the flap.

8. Embellish the flap or leave plain as is appropriate. Monograms or stitched stripes might look right.

9. Attach Velcro® dots to appropriate places.

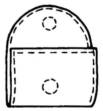

10. Insert belt through back slits of purse to wear.

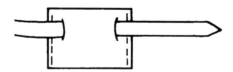

Fused Obi Sash

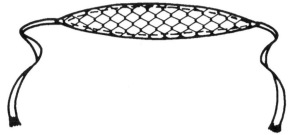

Made of fabric or suede, the Fused Obi Belt is always a popular belt. This style is especially appropriate in the heavier synthetic suedes. See also the Fleece-Core Obi on page 49.

1. Cut two midsection layers and two layers of paper-backed fusible web exactly the same, approximately the size of your waist.

2. Make two ties. These can be strips of suede, suede- or fabric-covered cord, fabric tubes that are stitched and turned, a combination of suede and fabric, ribbons, or even a jute-type cording. Make the ties long enough to overlap in back, come around to the front, and tie in a front bow or knot.

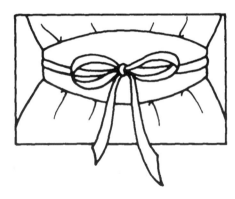

Non-Ravelly Materials

1. If both layers are non-ravelly fabric or suede, fuse paper-backed fusible web to the wrong side of front midsection. See the paper-backed fusible web package for heat setting and pressing time. Be sure to protect suede with a press cloth.

2. Remove paper backing and place midsection pieces wrong sides together.

3. Insert ends of the ties between the midsection layers and pin.

4. Steam press to fuse together layers and ties.

5. Edgestitch midsection, securing ties.

Ravelly Materials

A fabric that ravels needs 1/4" seams on all sides for finished edges.

1. Cut two midsection pieces, adding 1/4" seam allowances. Possibly use two different fabrics so the belt is reversible and you have two belts in one.

2. Cut two pieces fusible interfacing without the seam allowances.

3. Press fusible interfacing to the wrong side of midsections.

4. Right sides together, stitch 1/4" seam on top and bottom edges of midsections, leaving a small opening at each end to insert ties and to turn right side out.

5. Turn; press ends flat. Fold raw ends to the inside.

6. Insert tie ends into openings and pin.

7. Edgestitch midsection, securing ties.

Tie Borders

You may also stitch on a bound edge whose ends form ties. Use ravelly or non-ravelly materials for the midsection. Do not add a seam allowance.

1. Cut two matching midsection layers and one matching layer in fusible web. With midsections wrong sides together, insert fusible web, and fuse as one.

2. Use 1"- to 1-1/4"-wide binding if binding is ravelly and needs a seam allowance. Use 1/2"- to 3/4"-wide suede or non-ravelly fabric binding.

3. Cut one binding strip the length of the top edge of the midsection plus the length of two ties. Cut second strip of binding the length of bottom edge of midsection.

4. Fold binding strips in half lengthwise;

press. For ravelly fabric, open out and press under 1/4" seam allowance on each edge.

5. Enclose bottom edge of midsection with short binding strip; pin. Edgestitch top edge of binding.

6. To find center of belt, fold midsection in half. Mark at top with pin. Mark center of long binding strip.

7. Enclose top edge of midsection, matching centers and covering raw ends of bottom binding; pin. Continue folding rest of strip in half lengthwise; pin.

8. Edgestitch bottom edge along entire length of binding, creating ties and enclosing top edge of midsection.

Ribbon Belts

Wide ribbon can also make a lovely belt. Fuse two layers with fusible web or, to stiffen even more, fuse layers of fusible craft interfacing between ribbon layers. I'll show you how to make one using satin ribbon, which looks marvelous on a dressy outfit. It ravels out nicely at the ends to make a bow with a fringe. Instead of the bow, consider a rhinestone buckle from the notions department or a glittery pin from your jewelry box.

Supplies

- Heavy satin ribbon—twice your waist measurement plus a few inches for overlap; 25" for bow and holding piece
- Fusible web (like Stitch Witchery®)
- Fusible craft interfacing (optional)
- Hook and eye
- Matching thread

How to Make a Fused Ribbon Belt

1. Cut one length of ribbon twice your waist measurement plus a few inches for overlap.

2. Cut strip of fusible web the same width as ribbon and half as long.

3. If you need to "beef up" belt, cut a strip of fusible craft interfacing and fuse to wrong side of ribbon.

4. To make the ends of these ribbon-type belts neat with a professional-looking finish, don't cut the ribbon in half before fusing. Fold the ribbon in two crosswise, wrong sides together.

5. Insert fusible web between ribbon layers. Press to fuse.

6. The folded, uncut end has a smooth finish. Sew closure on this end.

7. Attach bow to other end of fused belt (see below). Conceal raw ends of belt between layers of small loop that covers bow midsection. Sew on hook to fasten at waist.

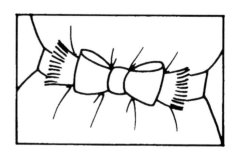

How to Make a Fringed Bow

1. Cut one length of ribbon 20" long.

2. Loop in half and stitch together 4" from ends.

3. Flatten out so stitched area is in center.

4. Wrap another small ribbon piece around the loop. Use an approximately 5" piece, depending on the ribbon width. A wider ribbon requires more length to go around.

5. Turn under the raw edge of this piece and hand stitch together, making sure that stitches do not go through to the belt itself.

6. Ravel ends of bow 3/4" to fringe.

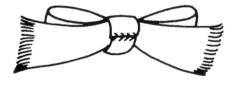

Ideas for Ribbon Belts

• Grosgrain ribbon is a slightly more casual look than satin, and a perfect way to add a splash of bright color to a linen or other plain fabric dress.

• Several bright accent colors might be even better in a striped ribbon or one you stripe yourself by stitching narrow ribbons onto a wide base of ribbon or of the dress fabric.

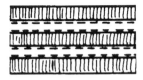

• If your machine has a bridging stitch to attach different widths of ribbons, suede strips, laces, etc., lay them side by side rather than appliquéing one on the other. Various stitch patterns might accomplish this. Experiment on your machine.

• While you're checking out the store's ribbon supplies, you might also consider velvet ribbons, the plaid taffetas, polka dots, or woven floral ribbons with lacy edges. These could be especially appealing used as sashes on little girls' dresses. The ribbons come in an enormous array of colors and widths. Some of these are so beautiful you'll find yourself buying ribbon first, then searching for fabric for a dress to go with it.

Little Bits

(vertical left) I repeated colors from the silk print in the suede stripes. The largest piece in the whole belt (the print end) is only 4" x 16".

(vertical right) Only a narrow wedge of the navy suede was available, and at one end it tapered down to 1/2" wide. I cut the leopard print wide enough for the underside lining so that it wrapped all around, almost touching, its edges together at the center on top. Then I fused the small suede scrap to bridge the gap, stitched it in place, and added a large front tab with small buttons.

(horizontal top) The red print remaining from a blouse was in a few small pieces, so I used red suede shapes to fill in the gaps.

(horizontal bottom)I fused pre-pleated poly-ester print to fleece to hold the pleats in place. A suede overlay gave it a finished, store-bought touch.

Fasteners for Stiff Belts

Stiff belts must all have some means of fastening. Although many use a simple hook and eye, a button and buttonhole, or a one-set-size fastener, think about the wisdom of this. If you frequently go up and down an inch or two in size, you really need the adjustability you get with a buckle and several eyelets, or hook-and-loop tape. Consider the many fasteners suggested and choose what is best for your fabrics and your personal comfort.

Eyelets in Stiff Belts

Stiff belts usually have holes or eyelets punched in them to hold a prong. I find the easiest way to punch holes is to use the tool for applying grippers. It easily and neatly punches a small hole, sufficient for the prong. If the fabric is not suede or leather, it is necessary to machine stitch an eyelet.

To allow for the differences in your waist size from morning to night, before and after dinner, etc., it is probably a good idea to punch two or three holes, 1" apart. When these holes are on a belt with a stationary prong, the hole end of the belt wraps under the buckle end against your body. Holes are, therefore, close to the end.

If the buckle has a movable prong on a center shaft, the belt slides through the buckle and its end shows on the topside. It is then necessary to have enough space between holes and tip to look right in the fastened position.

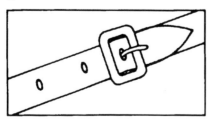

Buckles With Prongs

In buckles with prongs one end of the belt must be attached to the buckle. Cut a hole for the prong to go through. If this buckle will be used exclusively with one belt, wrap the end around the buckle shaft, then machine stitch in place. Remember when cutting out the belt to allow the extra length needed for this process.

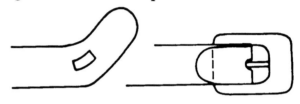

If the buckle will be transferred between belts, secure Velcro® strips to unsnap rather than permanently stitching the buckle. Apply these with Velcro® glue (both products available in notions departments). If glue won't hold on material, stitching is necessary.

Two-Piece Buckles With Clamp

There are also two-piece buckles that attach to the belt by means of a saw-tooth clamp. You may find it necessary to fuse a third layer between the two suede layers (on the ends only) to beef up the belt for a secure hold. Extra little scraps of suede will do this job, but remember to put a piece of fusible web both under and over that little scrap so the ends are all firmly fused.

Skirt Hooks

It is also possible to eliminate the need for a buckle by attaching large metal skirt hooks to attractively cut ends. Hand stitch-

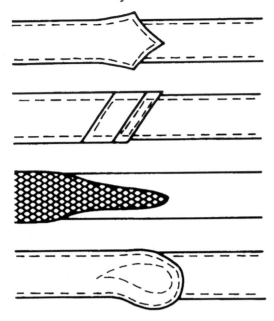

ing to the fused layers of suede is not easy however, and this may be better used on fabric belts. Possibly using the Velcro® strips is the easier way and also allows more adjustability.

Elongated Hooks

An elongated fastener I found in a notions department works almost like a screen door hook. A little metal half-ball has a large

hole on one side for the hook to attach, a little shank on the underside to sew on the belt. The hook half also has a little shank underneath to sew onto the opposite end of the belt. This type fastener definitely belongs in front. Putting it at your back waist would be uncomfortable when leaning back in a chair.

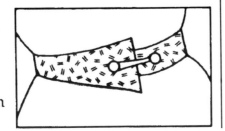

Underlap Loops With Wedge

For this fastener cut a hole in the overlapped end. The underlapped end has a little loop of either a strip of the belt material or a cording.

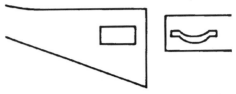

If your waistline measurement is erratic, stitch a succession of loops for adjustability.

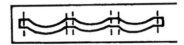

Overlap the belt ends so a loop comes up through the hole. Insert a wedge—it is both functional and decorative.

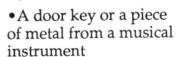

Some ideas for the wedge:

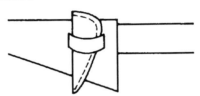

• An interesting piece of wood found on a country stroll

• A door key or a piece of metal from a musical instrument

• A lovely long narrow shell, the beachcomber's treasure

• If you can't unearth an interesting object, make a wedge, as described on page 13, by sewing something inside a fold of suede (maybe a long metal screw).

• Make another type of wedge: Simply cut a triangle of suede, glue part of its surface, and roll it up into a crescent or cornucopia the same as you'd do with yeast dough when making rolls.

Embellishing Stiff Belts

Embellish stiff belts in ways similar to the treatments on soft belts. Think in advance whether it would be easier to add the extra materials before or after fusing layers together. If the embellishment is flat and machine stitched, adding to a single layer in advance might be better. If the decoration is bulky or chunky, add it later.

See *Embellishing Soft Belts* on page 18 for more ideas for embellishing stiff belts.

Asymmetric Closures

Try an asymmetric effect on contour belts if this is flattering to your body. This off-balance treatment fools the eye and makes a waistline appear smaller than it really is.

Stitchery or a contrast in textures may accent this further and produce a really interesting belt. Throughout the book are many other ideas that could apply, and that enhance the appearance of your belt and your body.

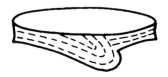

Collage With Mini-Pompons

Lay down yarns on the end piece first, then lay strips of suede in blending colors. Embellish with a few buttons, or mini-pompons made of the same yarn.

How to Make Mini-Pompons

This technique makes a little rosette. A couple of these hand stitched on the piece are pretty.

1. Lay a 4" piece of yarn on a knitting needle, slim pencil, or other thin, long object.

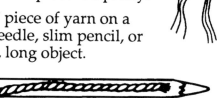

2. Holding one end of the yarn and needle, wind another length of yarn around about 30 times and cut off.

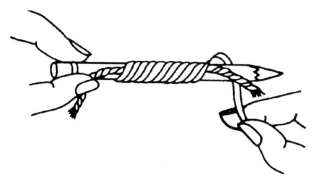

3. Carefully take the ends of the original 4" yarn and bring together, tying in a knot as it is pulled off the needle.

Couching

In the trims department, find about eight or ten exquisite braids, cords, or ropes, all dressy in feeling, all seeming to belong together. Buy a yard of each cord to make

seed-pearl strand

pewter metallic

pink metallic

slate-gray silk

blue-gray silk

pearl-gray silk

burgundy silk

silver metallic

charcoal silk

lavender silk

sure you have plenty. One possibility is to use the trapunto design on page 56. Use one of these cords attached in a wavy line throughout the length of the belt to set a design in the same way as the trapunto design was developed.

Then fill in the curvy spaces with all the other cords. Stitch or glue these cords to the fabric belt, filling in the spaces completely with an absolutely wonderful whimsy.

Fusing Yarn and Ribbon in Shapes

A combination of yarn and ribbon floss of the same color go perfectly with the suede background. (See page 41.)

1. Cut an interesting shape of paper-backed fusible web and fuse it on the upper layer center. Peel off the paper.

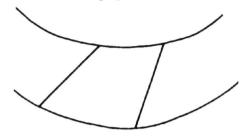

2. Pin this area to the ironing board, placing pins close together across top and bottom of shape. Lace the ribbon floss between the pins.

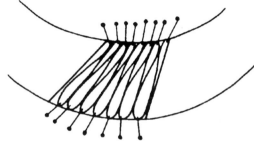

3. Fuse and remove pins.

4. Repeat a few stripes in the opposite diagonal with the yarn. Trim off excess yarn and ribbon ends and finish the belt.

Cutwork

The cutwork mentioned in the soft belt section (see page 18) might work even better with the stiffened belt, Velcro® dots forming a closure under the design.

Spinning A Yarn

Yarns lend texture, as well as blending or softening lines.

I'm not a knitter or weaver, but I have an on-going life-long love affair with yarns. In a yarn shop I find that whole wall of beautiful colors and textures much more than this mere mortal can resist. If I walk through one of these magical doors, I will not walk out empty-handed. Some of the offerings are gorgeous, but if I read "enough for a whole sweater," I retreat to the skeins or balls which are considerably smaller. I will be using this yarn only as an embellishment on a garment, belt, or bag. It is, therefore, sensible to get the small quantity which will actually be used, without needlessly building up a big stash. A fabric stash for a sewer is reasonable (no matter that it develops into warehouse proportions). A yarn stash for a non-knitter is really absurd.

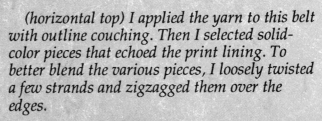

(horizontal top) I applied the yarn to this belt with outline couching. Then I selected solid-color pieces that echoed the print lining. To better blend the various pieces, I loosely twisted a few strands and zigzagged them over the edges.

(horizontal bottom) Fusing yarn in shapes is easy (see page 39). Here I chose a combination of yarn and ribbon floss of the same color to go perfectly with the suede background. I hand-sewed carved goat bones from Africa on top to complete the belt.

(vertical left) Similar to the previous idea, this belt has the yarns laid on the end piece first, then overlaid with strips of suede in blending colors.

(vertical right) A final embellishment on any belt might be a few buttons or mini-pompons made of the same yarn. These pompons are formed over a knitting needle or pencil (see page 38), which forms a pretty little rosette.

41

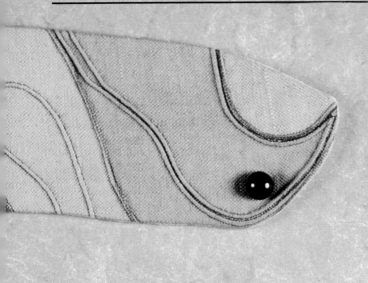

Fleece-Core Belts

(top to bottom) An abalone shell furnished the inspiration for the trapunto-stitched design trailing down the length of this belt. Nature punched the holes in the shell through which satin cord is woven, attaching the shell to the belt.

Twin-needle stitching accents and supplements the printed design of this linen fabric. The design turned out to resemble a bird...so I added a big shiny button "eye."

Two layers of wool surround a fleece core, stitched and turned right side out. Rows of stitching fill in the space for an interesting composition.

Similar to the belt above it, this one has some of the machine-stitched spaces filled with hand-stitched bugle and seed beads.

Any fabric can be used for a belt. Here the stitching is done on faux suede, the end enclosing a metal ring for firmness.

43

Fleece-Core Belts

More than a decade ago fusible webs came on the market, allowing the fusing together of two or more layers of faux suede or other fabrics. Any time a new product becomes available, it enhances techniques or makes the previously impossible possible for the home sewer. Before long, the web had been improved by adding a paper backing. Paper-backed fusible web is the product that prompted this whole section of fused belts with fleece cores.

The newest form is fusible fleece. While you could use this product, I don't use fusible fleece often because the fleece is cut to the exact size of the finished belt yet I also need the fusible agent on the part of the fabric that wraps over the fleece.

Three different belts are presented in this section: a Basic Fleece-Core Belt, an Obi, and a Stitched-and-Turned Belt. The Basic Fleece-Core Belt uses two layers of fleece, a Velcro® closure, and topstitching to hold the layers together. The Obi Belt uses only one layer of fleece and ties for fasteners. The Stitched-and-Turned Belt uses one layer of fleece, has layers stitched right sides together then turned right sides out, and uses buckles or any of the fasteners described under *Soft Belts*. See page 10.

Trims can be anything of your choice as suggested by the belt patterns and the fabrics you use. Fair game includes any decorative object that can be attached by fusing, gluing, sewing, or pinning, such as buckles, buttons, beads, sequins, pins. Accent fabrics, leathers, suedes, cords, and braids then make it uniquely yours. The fashion fabric and trims you choose will determine whether this is casual or elegant, for day or night. Personal variables will make each a completely different belt, resulting in an infinite number of possibilities.

Basic Fleece-Core Belt

Supplies

- 1/4 yard flat polyester fleece or craft felt (to make two strips 3" wide and 6" longer than waist measurement)
- 1 to 1-1/4 yard paper-backed fusible web
- 1/8 yard 45" fashion fabric or synthetic suede
- 1/8 yard 45" lining fabric
- 6" strip Velcro® hook and loop tape—more if waist size is unknown. Do not use the type with a sticky back as this complicates machine stitching.

Prepare the Pattern

1. On paper draw this belt pattern to full size. The total length will be the waist

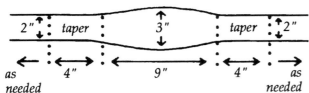

measurement plus a 6" overlap. If this will be a gift for an unknown size, make a larger overlap for greater adjustability.

2. Cut the center front midsection 3" wide, suitable for most people, but vary this width for personal taste.

3. Taper the belt narrower on either side down to a straight 2" across the back so that adjusted large or small, the overlap works out.

The shorter-waisted you are, the more you might want to narrow these widths. There is nothing sacred about when you taper or how wide the belt should be. Decide what's best for your figure.

Prepare the Fleece

1. Fold the fleece lengthwise.

2. Pin the pattern to the double thickness and cut the two layers at once to ensure exact duplicates.

3. Raise the end of one fleece layer, and with a fabric marker make a little mark on each layer. This will later help you fit the correct ends of the two layers together.

Fuse the Fusible Web

1. Fold the paper-backed fusible web in half lengthwise.

2. Pin the pattern to this double layer .

3. Cut, adding about 5/8" seam allowance on all sides.

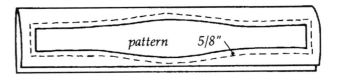

4. On the ironing board place the uncut piece of fashion fabric *wrong side up.*

5. Position on top one layer of paper-backed fusible web *rough (fusible) side down.* The paper side will be on top, protecting your iron as you fuse it to the fabric.

6. Set your iron to *synthetic.* Fuse web to fabric following manufacturer's instructions.

7. Cut out fabric at the edge of the fusible web. Repeat this process on the *wrong side* of the lining layer.

8. Peel off the paper backing and discard or save for future use as a pattern.

Fuse the Fleece

1. Place fashion fabric on ironing board *fusible side up.*

2. Center a layer of fleece, *marked side up.*

3. At each end fold fabric over fleece and fuse in place.

4. Pin these ends to ironing board, stretching belt out to hold it tautly in place.

5. Fold over top and bottom seam allowances, clipping at tapered curve if necessary.

6. To fuse edges of seam allowance, push pins at a steep angle toward edges of belt into board padding to hold fabric temporarily in place. Run edge of iron over outer folds to fuse flat.

Fleece layer with fabric edges folded over

7. Remove all pins and fuse thoroughly on both sides, using a press cloth if fabric is delicate. Repeat this process with the lining layer.

Make Basic Fleece-Core Belt Fastener

1. To create the anchor that keeps the belt end flat on the body, cut a 4" x 1-1/2" rectangle of paper-backed fusible web.

2. Fuse web to the *wrong side* of fashion fabric scrap.

3. Trim off excess fabric and peel off the paper backing.

4. Fold the long sides to the center and finger press in place.

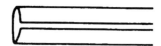

5. Fold again and fuse with the iron.

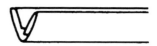

6. Edgestitch both long sides on machine.

7. About 1/4" from one end of the lining layer, with the *fabric side up*, underlap the anchor end and stitch in place.

8. With scissors cut round corners on the 6" long soft (loop side) strip of Velcro®.

9. Pin to lining layer 1/2" from end and machine stitch in place.

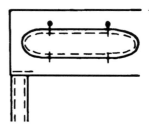

Join the Belt Layers

Note: Embellish the fashion fabric layer now if raw edges of embellishments must be concealed between layers. See embellishment suggestions described below and also under *Soft Belts.* See page 18.

1. Now join the two belt layers. Matching marked fleece sides, pin all edges in place.

2. Beginning at point A, which is about 1" from belt end, stitch all around belt to corner B. Use a matching thread or if a print makes this too difficult, use invisible monofilament nylon thread.

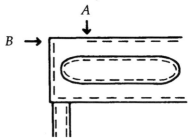

3. Bring the anchor over the Velcro® and insert its end in the opening between points A and B. Leave the anchor slightly loose against the fabric to permit space for the other belt end to slip through.

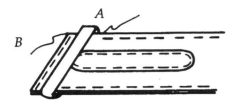

4. With the belt in a rolled position to keep the anchor loop out of the way, machine stitch the small opening closed (B to A), attaching the anchor end between the belt layers in the process.

5. Cut the hook strip of Velcro® down to 1-1/2", rounding all corners. At the opposite belt end, *fabric side up*, pin, then stitch the Velcro® in place.

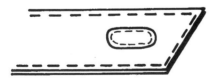

6. To wear the belt, slide the hook end through the anchor, keeping a finger handy to prevent catching too soon. Adjust comfortably at waist and smooth to seal Velcro®.

Contoured Fleece-Core Belt

A straight belt like the Basic Fleece-Core Belt rides from your waist on up and creates an illusion of a shorter upper body and longer legs. A contour belt starts at your waistline and extends below it, thus lengthening your upper body while shortening your legs. If a contour belt is more flattering for you than a straight belt, double the fabric, fleece and paper-backed fusible web amounts. It takes about twice as much material to curve the belt. The places marked X will be waste yardage. You can, of course, save scraps to add to another project.

Front Closure Fleece-Core Belt

Try fastening the Basic Fleece-Core Belt in front instead of in back. Follow the instructions for the Basic Fleece-Core Belt—the only differences follow.

1. Vary the width of the two belt ends for a flattering asymmetric effect.

2. Cut the wider end square, round, or whatever shape pleases you.

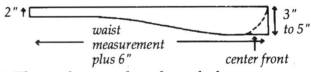

3. The anchor needs to be only large enough to accommodate the narrow end.

4. Stitch the anchor to the lining side of the wide end.

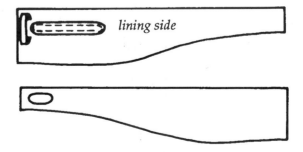

5. The wide end of the belt overlaps the narrow end when worn.

Obis

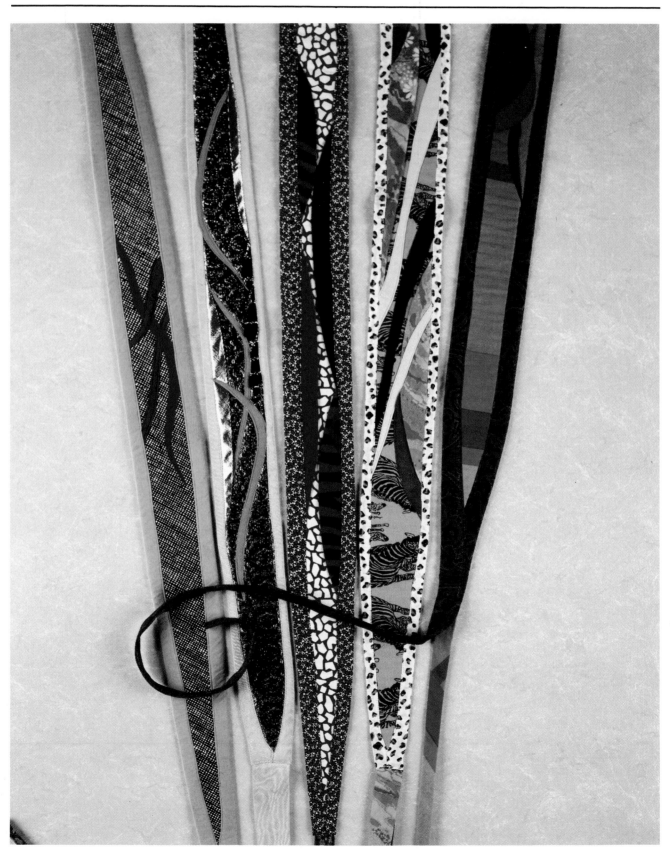

Shirley Adams' Belt Bazaar

The Fleece-Core Obi

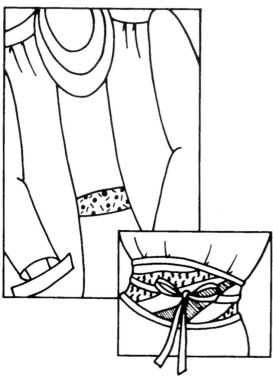

This obi ties in front after double wrapping the waist. It fits any size waist, wrapping once or twice, depending on the waist size. For a larger waistline, it wraps once and ties in back. It can be any width the wearer desires.

A tiny waist can look terrific in an enormously wide belt, but this width might be unflattering to a larger waistline. However, for those who think their waists cannot handle a belt, showing a belt in the center of an open jacket or sweater that partially conceals the sides can advantageously hint at a small waistline.

Part of the fascination of making these particular belts is in discovering fabric scraps from the distant past up to the present that coordinate so beautifully. If you include in this belt a bit of fabric from garments you wear presently, it helps create united ensembles and you will be able to wear the belt with more than one outfit.

I like to form the lining, binding, and ties from complementary colors and prints, then use another print in the same colors for the upper layer fabric. To contrast with the upper layer fabric, I cut embellishment suede pieces of similar colors in curved shapes (see page 57). These are stitched down before sewing the binding in place.

Supplies

- 1/4 yd of 45"-wide fabric for the belt front side

- 1/8 yd to 1/4 yd of 45"-wide fabric (depending on desired belt width). This is for lining which becomes front edge binding—an important element of belt's embellishment.

- Polyester fleece 3" to 5" wide and 40" or so long

- Paper-backed fusible web

- Harmonizing fabric strips or cords for ties 20" or so long

- Embellishments, such as other fabrics, small pieces of synthetic suede, cords, yarns, or any trim that seems to belong. Look through your fabric scraps treasury to find just the right additions. With color as the coordinating factor, large and small prints, solids, plaids, or stripes may all be mixed successfully.

Note: The ambiguity of size requirements in the supply list allows for differences in body size, as well as in personal preference.

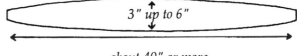

3" *up* to 6"

about 40" or more

Ties stitched to each end will further extend the length.

Cut and Fuse the Obi

1. Cut one layer of fleece the desired size and shape of finished belt.

2. Cut two layers of paper-backed fusible web the same shape.

3. With an iron set on synthetic, fuse one layer of fusible web to each side of fleece.

4. Peel off paper cover from one side of fused belt form.

5. Position it, fusible side down, against the *wrong side* of the fashion fabric being used for face side of belt. Press to fuse in place.

6. Trim the fabric down to the edge of the fleece, which is the exact belt edge. No seam allowances are added.

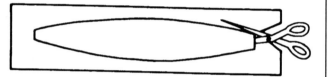

7. Peel off the other paper backing and position the fusible side down to the *wrong* side of the fabric that will form the belt lining and binding. Be sure there is 1" or a little more fabric extending beyond the belt edges.

8. Fuse in place. Trim excess fabric if desired, but it is all right if the 1" at center enlarges to 1-1/2" or 2" at ends since the binding need not be a uniform width.

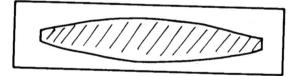

Make Ties and Finish the Obi

1. Make one or two ties, or whatever number is desired for each end. I used two at each end. Make ties by cutting harmonizing fabrics approximately 24" long and 2-1/2" wide at one end, tapering narrower at the other end to perhaps 1-1/2" wide. You may also use commercial cords.

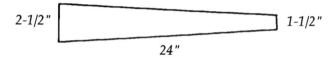

2. Fold these ties in half lengthwise, right sides together, and stitch a 1/4" seam the entire length.

3. Turn right side out with a loop turner.

4. Tuck the raw edge of narrow end inside tube 1/2" or so to finish.

5. Press the extended lining fabric edges to the belt face side, folding up at heavy edge of fleece, starting with the two short ends.

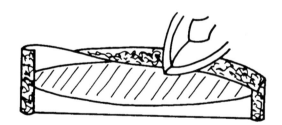

6. Lay the wide raw-edged ends of the ties on top of the belt ends, concealed under the fold-over binding. Pin in place.

7. Tuck under raw binding edges of top and bottom curves of obi and press in place.

Note: Add optional embellishment at this point *before* any sewing takes place. See pages 56-57 for embellishment ideas.

8. Pin as necessary along the rest of binding, and edgestitch in place to complete the obi.

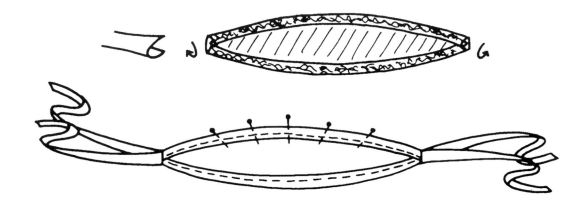

Stitched-and-Turned Fleece-Core Belts

This belt can be made from any woven or knit fabric—maybe the same as the garment with which it will be worn. Or add a textural contrast, such as a belt made in shiny satin the same color as a matte crepe dress. I especially like to use mock trapunto as an embellishment on these kinds of belts.

If you make the upper belt layer slightly smaller than the back lining layer, when you stitch the edges of the two layers, the larger lining will look like piping.

Supplies
- 1/2 yd of 45"-wide fabric
- Fusible or non-fusible fleece
- Matching thread
- Matching Velcro® (optional)
- Hook and eye (optional)
- Buckle (optional)
- Pattern paper
- Water-soluble pen
- Embellishments including embroidery thread, silky cord, fabric appliqués, beads, sequins, and any findings

Cut and Fuse the Belt
1. Decide on the belt's shape and width. Cut a scrap of fabric or paper the anticipated size and hold it around your waist in front of a mirror to determine its effect. The amount of overlap for fastening will depend on whether a hook and eye will be sewn on or a buckle added. Allowing some adjustability will make the belt more comfortable.

2. Cut two layers of fabric the necessary size plus small (1/4") seam allowances all the way around.

3. Cut a layer of fleece the exact size of the finished belt (without seam allowances). This fleece, usually polyester, is sold from a bolt in the interfacing department. It is available in thin or thick lofts, depending on the desired effect. You might use two layers for extra firmness. Polyester fusible fleece is also available.

4. Center fleece on the wrong side of one fabric layer. Pin in place and stitch around edge to hold in place, or fuse fusible fleece with iron.

5. Right sides together, pin other fabric layer to the first layer and stitch around outside of fleece, stitching only the two fabric layers together. Leave about a 2"

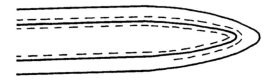

open space in order to turn the belt right side out. Use a wooden spoon handle or a yardstick as a turning tool.

6. Press. By hand, whip together the open space.

Embellish and Finish the Belt

1. I like to use mock trapunto on these belts (see page 56), but you can use any method, as long as you have a way to hide the raw ends of any added material (unless, of course, you like the texture of raw ends).

2. Attach Velcro®, hook and eye, or buckle.

3. Depending on the fabric and the technique, further embellish with fabric appliqués in some of the shapes and spaces. Silky cord coiled and stitched can either outline or fill spaces. If intended for evening wear, fill in with bugle beads, seed pearls, sequins or paillettes, or a jeweled pin. Any findings can prove fascinating and "make" an otherwise rather undistinguished outfit.

Embellishing Fleece-Core Belts

Your belt fabric suggests the embellishment it needs. Let your fabric speak. It won't say the same thing to every listener, and that is why an infinite variety is possible within any of the design ideas offered here. Begin with an interesting fabric, and a belt almost makes itself. The more elaborate the fabric, the more simple the treatment should be; the more plain the fabric, the more it asks you to add designs to it. Have fun with the linings too, making them as appealing as the exterior.

Any fabric, thick or thin, woven or knit, when fused to the fleece core, becomes firm and suitable for embellishment. Also check the embellishment ideas under *Soft Belts* and *Stiff Belts*. I use all of those ideas on Fleece-Core Belts, especially appliqué, but I don't have space here to repeat ideas.

I love to embellish Fleece-Core Belts so much that most of the Design Pages in this book are of this type. Be sure to read how I thought through each belt.

Windows

1. After you fuse paper-backed fusible web to the fabric's wrong side and before you fuse the fleece to it, draw some interesting shapes on the paper and cut out the "windows."

2. Choose some interesting fabric to be seen through the windows. Stripes, prints, or contrasting colors harmonize or accent.

3. Pleat or otherwise texture this fabric for still another dimension.

4. Cut pieces of fleece a little larger than the window openings. Fuse the "scenes" to these pieces of fleece.

5. Position the scenes under the open windows and pin in place.

6. Edgestitch (if suede or leather) or satin stitch (if a ravelly fabric) around windows, permanently joining them to the scene. Then finish the belt in the usual way.

- Use pleated silk, in both the belt lining and as the scene in these windows.

- Cut windows in shapes to suit print design that shows through. For example, cut snakey-shaped windows in reptile-looking fabric. Add rows of stitching to repeat window shapes.

Create Textures for Windows

Manipulate fabric to create texture under the windows.

1. Accordion pleat a thin linen print fabric, and press pleats in place.

2. Pin one end to the ironing board, fan the loose end out and press again, creating shallower folds.

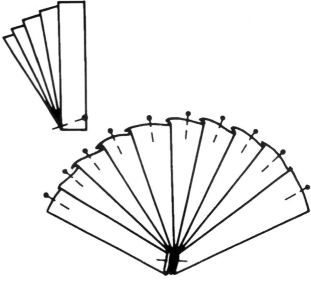

3. Fuse wrong side to fleece, then position under windows; edgestitch.

Windows

Cutting windows into your belt opens many possibilities. Choose some interesting fabric to be seen through the window. Stripes, prints, or contrasting colors harmonize or accent. Pleat or otherwise texture this fabric for still another dimension.

There are always little scraps left over from any sewing, but possibly not enough to cover an entire belt. Small pieces showing through windows coordinate the belt with the fabric of the outfit.

The framework fused over or around a window covers the raw edges and gives a finished look. You can use satin stitches to cover the raw edges of the framework window. If you use faux suede, the satin stitching is unnecessary—straight edgestitching is sufficient and faster.

(on top) I pleated silk, the same fabric used in the belt lining, as the scene in these windows.

(left) A cotton zebra print is the scene out the windows, which I placed to suit the zebras showing through. Stitched rows repeat window shapes. The upper belt layer is slightly smaller than the black lining layer. When edges of the two layers are stitched, the larger lining looks like piping.

(middle) I accordion-pleated a thin linen print fabric and pressed it in place. While a pin held one end to the ironing board, I fanned the loose end out and pressed again. Then I fused wrong side to fleece and positioned it under windows to edgestitch. Because both red and burgundy are in the print, I cut the end piece of the belt in red, while the remainder of the belt is burgundy. My ulterior motive in adding this red was to legitimize the red shoes and bag worn with the print dress.

(right) The reptile-looking jacquard weave of the lining fabric told me to cut snakey-shaped windows.

Mock Trapunto

Traditional trapunto is a method of stitching channels, then pulling yarn through them for a three-dimensional effect. Mock trapunto stitching uses fleece as padding between the layers to give the same raised effect. I usually make a Stitched-and-Turned Fleece-Core Belt for this technique.

1. For the trapunto effect, either design a pattern and mark with a water-soluble pen (which will later disappear with a touch of moisture) or improvise as you stitch. Hand-quilting stencils are also a good source of design.

2. Use the presser foot as a guide in determining width between stitched rows. The pattern may be straight parallel lines or any fanciful design.

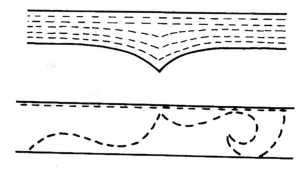

3. The first row stitched provides shapes for repeated stitching. Then just keep stitching to your heart's content until all areas are stitched in a way that pleases you. This may sound ridiculous, but I can't tell you how relaxing this mindless stitching can be.

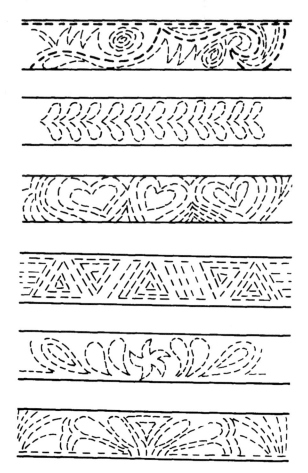

You can think of more designs than these few but let these serve as starting points.

Curved Fabric Collage

Because these football-shaped pieces of fabric are cut on the bias, they can be curved and manipulated. The raw edges are hidden by the binding or seam at the edge. I like to use them for Obi Belts, where the embellishment is worked before the binding is stitched down.

1. Cut the embellishing fabrics in the shape shown and on the bias so that they can curve and be pressed into the desired shape.

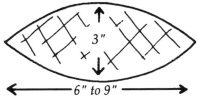

2. Press these pieces in half lengthwise, and slightly stretch while steam pressing so that the fold becomes a curve—the raw edges close to straight-lined.

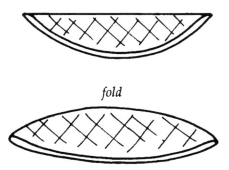

fold

3. Slide the raw edges under the binding of an Obi and pin in place. Complete the belt.

Appliqué

Suede Scraps

You can appliqué any fabric, but it's particularly easy on suede scraps because they don't have raw edges. I would like to say these are artistically cut suitable shapes, but I must admit they emerge from my suede scrap supply in these shapes. Anyone can be an artist with this fabric medium. It is merely a matter of trial and error. In the illustrations, I am working on an Obi Belt before the binding is stitched down.

Try various placements before pinning. Then topstitch when you arrive at a satisfying arrangement.

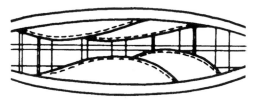

Narrow Suede Strips

This technique of topstitching narrow suede strips is possible because of the material's pliability.

1. Cut the strips in the shape shown, but stretch slightly into curves while edgestitching into place.

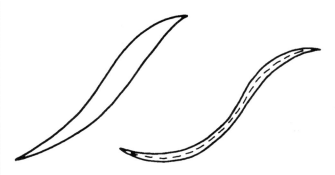

2. When doing this type of stitching, it is difficult to start at a point and progress away from it without getting the suede hung up under the presser foot. The easiest way is to begin stitching elsewhere and stitch up to the point. Leave the needle down in the fabric while lifting the presser foot. Pivot the fabric 180°, lower foot, and proceed. A small needle (10/70) works best with the synthetic suede.

3. Manipulate the strips either while sewing, or in advance by pinning or gluing to temporarily hold in place.

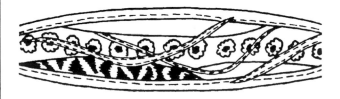

Corded Belts

(middle diagonal) After I made fabric tubes over upholstery welting, I braided six cords and affixed them to a fabric-covered D ring.

(right diagonal) Choose one print fabric to furnish the color scheme. Then mix any other woven or knit fabrics whose colors blend and make cords from them.

(horizontal) What could be simpler than three purchased cords of black, silver, and gold, loosely twisted and attached to a silver hook?

Corded Belts

Corded belts include a wide variety of roping. We'll first deal with what's available commercially plus what you can produce on your own. Then we'll move into how to twist, loop, braid, knot, or otherwise turn them into belts.

Commercially Available Cord

In the fabric shops you can purchase narrow silk cords with a satin sheen in a large assortment of colors. They also have medium and fat cording of cotton, rayon, jute, or wool. Most of these are sold by the yard from large spools. Sometimes fat, twisted, silken cord is sold as a piece with tassels on the ends. Similar ones are found in drapery and upholstery shops. Also available by the yard are leathers or fabrics sewn around an inner cotton core, as well as metallics and nighttime glitter. You might be pleasantly surprised to find exactly what you need to accent or blend with that special garment.

Also try the yarn shops. Yarns are gorgeous, soft, luxurious, with a breathtaking array of colors. The textures blend or contrast and range from smooth, glittery elegance to rugged, nubby earthiness. Look for yarns with contrasts in sizes and textures to produce a really interesting effect.

Loosely twisted linen or all manner of novelty yarns can become exciting components in an artistic collage. They're lovely teamed with gleaming metal fasteners or natural woods. You don't have to be a knitter to go into a yarn shop and find several types you can't resist buying to add to belts.

Spend some time in the various shops combining materials in different ways to find the look you need. How much yardage you buy depends on how the cords will be handled. Straight or slightly twisted will not take too much more for each length than the waist size. But if you are incorporating braiding, knotting, or "spaghetti bowl" techniques, those strands must be considerably longer.

Making Your Own Cord

Suede Strips

Make some cording of your own by cutting strips of suede. A rotary cutter is ideal for a quick, straight cutting job. Lean the rotary cutter against a metal or plastic ruler and cut straight lines. This is not only quicker and more accurate, but also much easier than trying the same thing with scissors. Think also if you want to cut the suede completely through, or if it would be better to leave ends intact to use as a bundle instead of individual strands.

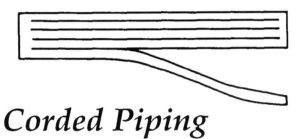

Corded Piping

Another cord to make involves long scraps of fabric sewn wrong sides together around a core such as upholstery welting or fat rug yarn. A raw seam allowance shows.

1. Use gluestick to temporarily hold the scraps in place.

2. Stitch close to cord using a zipper foot.

3. Trim edges near stitching line.

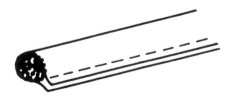

Spaghetti Cord

Spaghetti cord is cord covered with a fabric tube with the seam allowance inside the tube, unlike corded piping. Spaghetti cord is usually of a small diameter, similar to slip straps. Fabric of any sort works for spaghetti cord, but the slipperier that fabric is, the easier it will be to turn right side out. Cut on the bias if using woven fabric so that it falls more softly and smoothly into place. Fabric cut on the straight grain might finish out unattractively in little peaks or points everywhere it later curves. The exception to this is a knit fabric that gains greater stretch and smoothness by cutting on the crossgrain. Here's how.

Creating Bias Strips

When you need bias, only *true bias* cut on a 45° angle will do. Any other angle will pull and ripple and be unworthy of your efforts. To find the true bias, fold fabric diagonally so the selvage edge forms a right angle. The fold indicates the true bias.

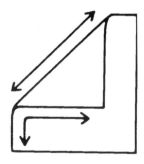

If you need a longer strip, join pieces, matching edges at the seam allowance, not at the ends of the strip.

A large quantity of bias can be mass-produced quickly with only one joining seam in this way:

1. Fold fabric to find bias direction and measure off enough length for as many pieces as you like.

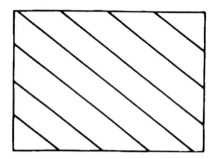

2. With a yardstick and fabric marking pen, draw parallel lines the desired width of each strip.

3. Fold fabric right sides together offsetting ends one strip and pin. Stitch a 1/4" seam and press it open.

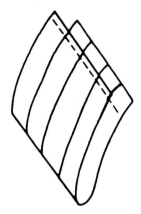

4. Start cutting on marked line and as you follow marked line, bias will fall away in one long continuous strip.

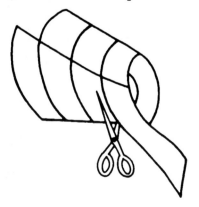

Covering Cord With Fabric

Turn bias into usable cord using white cotton or nylon cording in various thicknesses, carried in notions departments for this purpose and purchased by the yard.

1. Decide how much covered cord you need. Cut bias fabric to that length.

2. Begin with a cord *twice* the length needed.

3. Fold bias fabric right sides together over midpoint of cord. This leaves equal amounts of uncovered cord.

4. At middle of cord, stitch across end of fabric to anchor it, then stitch along the length of fabric using cording-zipper foot in order to stitch fairly close to cord. Use tiny stitches so thread is less likely to break when being turned.

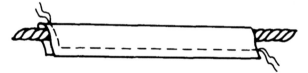

5. Hold the cord by the open end of the bias tube. With the other hand, begin to roll the fabric over the cord. A straight pin may be needed to begin the process, pinning point through fabric to pull, but avoiding pinning through cord.

6. Once the turning is begun, pull out the pin and use fingers (and probably fingernails) to complete the process, which turns easily and quickly.

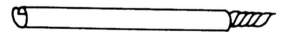

7. The finished right-side-out tube covers the formerly exposed cording. Cut off the newly exposed cording. You may prefer the alternative of using a fabric tube turner.

Making Corded Belts

Using cords, either a purchased type or ones you made of fabric-covered cores, let's do some simple twists. We'll first consider forming the belts, then think of the alternatives for fastenings.

An important decision in making cord belts is how to hold together, or anchor, multiple cords. Variations in this section describe making a center knot, stitching suede patches across the cords, and other techniques to hold the cords securely at center front. Other solutions include wrapping the cords at intervals and braiding.

Single Anchor Belts

In single anchor belts, cords are held together in only one place, usually at center front. The ideas range from simply looping cords together to sewing on appliquéd suede patches.

Loop Anchors

Looped Cords

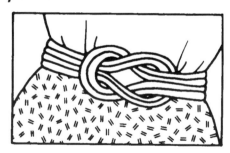

This cord belt involves four cords: two doubled around the right side of your body, two around the left. Simply loop these at the center front. All four of these can be the same color, or use two, three or four different colors. You're the designer, free to do as you like!

Front Knot

Make a large flat center knot, tapering to parallel ends. How about combining bias fabric cords and metallic roping?

Silk-Wrapped Loop

Wrap multiple color silk cording around an inner core. Tie in back. See *Multiple Anchors—Wrapped Groups* on page 65 for instructions on how to wrap the inner core with silk cord.

Yarn Loop

You can make a easy yarn belt that doesn't look simple. Casually loop, then wrap, loosely bundled yarns.

Patch Anchors

Suede Anchor I

1. Decorate a square of suede by appliquéing some snakeskin, couching a silk cord, or whatever you wish.

2. Cut another backing square in the same color and material.

3. Sandwich cords between the two squares and edgestitch.

4. Tie cord ends together with a knot on each end.

These ends can then be looped through each other to hold at back waist, or tied there in a knot. Look through the book for other back fastening ideas.

Suede Anchor II

1. Cut a piece of suede in the shape shown.

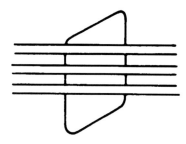

2. Lay cords on top.

3. Fold top and bottom corners of suede over cords using dabs of gluestick to hold everything in place temporarily.

4. Stitch between cords for an interesting effect as well as serving as an anchor to keep the cords firmly in place.

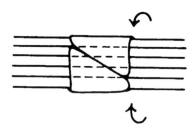

5. You can knot the back closing, the same as the previous belt. But if you think a knot in the middle of your back is uncomfortable to lean back on, stitch flat suede patches enclosing cord ends. Connect two suede ends with Velcro® or hooks and eyes.

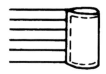

Ring Anchors

Bracelet With Knots

This belt works especially well with yarns and two brown wooden bracelets for rings. I used brown, beige, mostly neutral yarns with a touch of lavender and purple for a little surprise element and to make it blend with some of my wardrobe.

1. Begin by cutting many different yarns all the same length—about 5'.

2. Tie knots, perhaps at 1' intervals, to casually hold the group together.

3. Tie the two bracelets together with a single knot for starters. This creates the effect of a single buckle.

4. Twine yarn through the bracelets and tie the yarn ends either at the back of your waist, or bring back to the front.

Multiple Anchors

Wrapped Groups

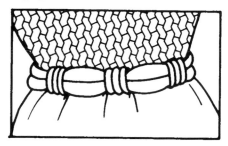

Leave two or three cords straight and bind them at intervals with narrower cords. Fat suede cords with shiny satin cord wrapping are an attractive choice.

1. To wrap cords, begin on the backside. Tie a knot in the satin cord for ballast. Hold it sideways between belt cords.

2. Wind satin around as much as you like. To finish off, tie a knot in the other end, tuck it under wrapping. You might put a dab of glue at either end to keep knots permanently in place, or thread a needle and take a couple of stitches to hold each end.

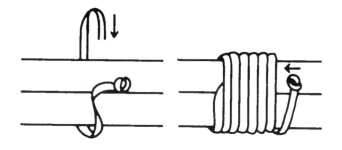

Woven Groups

Another way to use the silk cord is to weave it in and out of each belt cord. The effect will not be solid glossy silk in appearance like the simple wraps described in *Wrapped Groups,* but still binds together several cords in a flat belt.

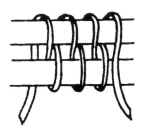

Ring Groups

Use small metal or plastic rings to achieve the flat belt effect. Thread the belt cords through the rings and group them at intervals. The rings will flatten sideways. Anchor them with a couple

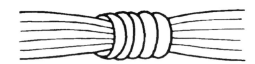

of hand stitches holding the first and last ring to the backside of the cords so the rings don't move.

Clamp Groups

In some craft or notions departments, you can find binding clamps to create a flat cord belt. These are like large decorative staples with side arms that bend under to surround several cords.

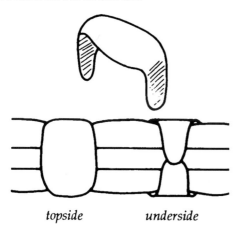

topside   *underside*

Knotted Groups

1. Using several textures in an interesting color combination, cut several 5' lengths of each type.

2. About every foot, tie the whole bunch in a knot to lightly hold it all together.

Braided Anchors

Simple Braiding

Everyone knows how to braid a simple three-strand braid. Maybe you've done it on a little girl's hair, or maybe on yeast dough in making some fancy bread or a coffee cake. This braid could be done with groups of differently textured yarns, or mixtures with suede, fabric, cording made of whatever pleases you or whatever you have on hand that matches or complements an outfit.

Complex Braiding

Some corded belts may seem complex, but once you analyze them carefully, anyone can do the weaving. This example has six different cords.

1. Start with cord #1 and follow it as it goes under, over, under.

2. Cord #2 then does the same thing, followed by #3 and so on. These are pictured loosely woven so that you can more easily figure it out.

3. Tighten these to form a solid belting.

6 5 4 3   2 1

4. This example is similar but with four cords instead of six. Notice as you follow one cord, then another, that the weaving technique is the very same.

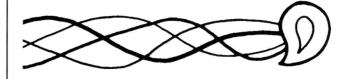

Fasteners for Cord and Yarn Belts

To make cord or yarn belts even more attractive, add a decorative end to the cord, or wrap and knot the ends around an interesting buckle. This is where found objects are particularly handy. Have you worn that bangle bracelet lately? Try it as a single buckle for a cord belt.

Mock Fastener

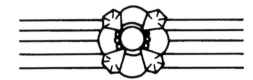

A quickie belt might be a 3-yard length of cord whose color goes with your dress.

1. Wrap it around and around your waist, tying the ends in a knot and tucking them underneath. I don't think I need to explain this advice, but it might be preferable to use this idea on a dress or a skirt, not through the belt loops of a pair of pants that you may need to remove quickly!

2. At the center front, as a mock fastener, simply attach a costume jewelry pin for a big effect.

Suede Fastener

Since multiple cord belts might be best fastened between end layers of suede, make a suede tab fastener for your belt.

1. Use several cords in assorted colors or all the same color.

2. Cut them to your waist size minus about 3".

3. Gluestick cord ends between layers of suede cut in two shapes, one a rectangle and the other with two tab ends.

4. Fuse, stitch around edges.

5. Punch holes in the tab end, and attach little buckles to the other end.

Loop Fasteners

Loop-Decorated Dangling Cords

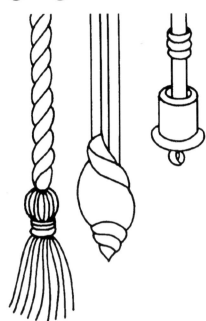

Long, dangling cord ends can be made attractive by adding a decorative object such as a tassel or shell. To wear it as a belt, simply fold the cord near the halfway mark, then loop the ends through the fold.

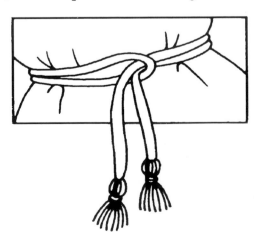

Dimension in Fabric

   Slight irregularities in cut from the original pattern can produce some interesting variations.

   Anytime there is some dimensional addition or greater thickness, it is better to design a straight belt rather than a contoured one. This is because the straight shape fits the body from the waist on up. The contoured belt curves below the waist. No woman needs any additional bulk in this tummy area!

(top left) I cut the center about 3" wider in a curve. Then I fused a second layer of suede to the center section only and machine-stitched all edges. Finally, I stitched the large buttons on to hold the fabric folds in place.

(bottom left) I cut the front 6" considerably wider than the rest of the belt, and gathered it up to fit the point which overlaps it. This is a simple but effective design.

(top right) I cut the midsection of the outer layer about 4" longer than the pattern. Every 1/2", I made a slash with a buttonhole cutter, for a total of 14 cuts. Lacing a suede-covered cord through the slashes, I drew up until it fit the original fleece and tied knots in the ends of that cord. Then I machine-stitched the belt together, except for that pleated midsection, which was joined by hand stitches.

(bottom right) This rhinestone buckle is strictly decorative, as the belt actually fastens in back. Similar to B, the center is cut extra wide, but also it splits and is about 12" longer. I folded that excess back, gathering it up to fit through the buckle, and hand-stitched it in place.

The same can be done on a cord that has both ends attached to one object, like this shell.

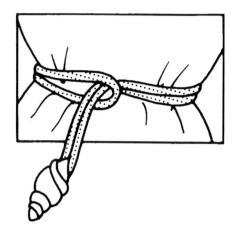

One-Piece Fasteners

How to Fasten a Single Buckle

Attach cords to wood, metal, or plastic objects, like this shiny silver paisley-shaped buckle purchased in a notions department.

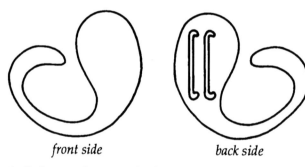

front side   *back side*

1. Select a fat tasseled cord that is long enough to go around your waist twice.

2. Fold almost in half, and push the fold end under the back brackets of the buckle.

3. Pull through to the other end so the tassels are near the bracket, but hanging down somewhat.

4. Wrap the fold end around the waist and loop over the metal hook.

The vertical lines of these hanging belts make you look taller, slimmer—the Greek goddess look.

Single Buckle With Bracket

1. Tie the loop end on the bracket in a half-hitch knot.

2. On the front side tie a knot on the hook end of the fastener. This same idea can be used on a lot of buckles. If the buckle has a middle brace, loop the cord fold around it.

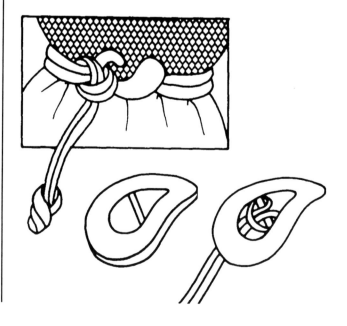

3. Then tie the end with the shell, knot, bead, tassel, or other object, in a knot on the other end of the buckle.

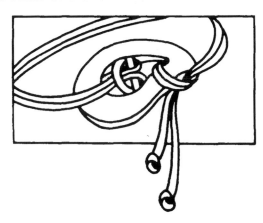

Buckle Without Bracket

If there is no middle bracket, as in this fat wood doughnut, loop folded end to secure and tie other end in a knot.

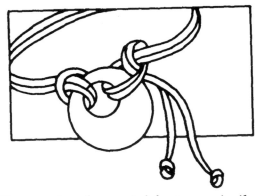

Treat a chunky metal fastener similarly: attach the loop to one hole; knot the ends to the other.

Weave Cord Through Found Object

A three-holed object like this burnished bronze might be flat, but can have those same cords woven through, hanging down through the center hole. If this cord doesn't stay in place without slipping, weave it the opposite way, and tie a knot on top of the center hole.

Twist Cord in Metal Anchor

A three-holed metal object makes a perfect anchor for cord or twisted yarns. Here is one twisting idea. There is nothing magic, or right or wrong, about the way this is looped around. It is merely an example to encourage you to try your hand at it. Experiment to see what you can come up with as you intertwine and knot yarn or cord through the metal.

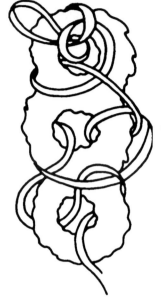

1. Begin by doubling a long length, 6' or so, of a few yarns.

2. Tie a knot around the metal at upper left to secure.

3. Loop and twist as the mood moves you. Allow your imagination to see this in several textured fuzzy yarns instead of just the simple double lines and it becomes something wonderful. The lower tail of yarns coming out of the metal will go around your waist and tie through that upper loop.

Two-Piece Buckle Fasteners

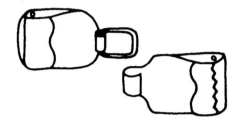

Many two-piece buckles on the market have ends with saw-tooth clamps. These will securely hold the cords if the cords are fat enough. If not, it may be necessary to sew the cord ends into suede patches, then insert these into the clamps. This isn't such a bad idea, as the suede holds the cord belt permanently together, and buckles can be interchangeable.

1. Gluestick cord ends between matching pieces of suede.

2. Fuse, stitch around edges.

Fancy Corded Belt

This is the corded belt I was wearing when I went shopping in the most exclusive shops in a large city (see page xi). It is a loosely braided belt.

What old necklaces do you still have that may lend just the right touch? How about those "twister" beads you bought when they were all the rage but now seem a little passé? Wood, ceramic, plastic, glass beads? Any chains to be used as belt cording? Do you have broken jewelry from yesteryear you've been meaning to fix, but never will get around to it? Take it apart and use the individual beads to sew on here and there. When a belt is this loosely twisted and unstructured, your collage must be mounted on something firm, such as a base belt of dress fabric.

This belt is a combination of about 15 – 20 strands of natural-colored linen yarn knotted together at ends. Fifteen strands of thin silk cord also tie in a knot. It also contains a 1-1/2" strip of suede shredded in straight lines by a rotary cutter, but ends left intact, and a strand of colored beads. All of these components are the same length, about 4" longer than the waist.

This type of belt can be the focal point of a costume, and definitely can be considered waistline jewelry. On a larger or smaller waist it can be lovely, especially if the colors are all soft, close blends. Make this for a simple linen dress, and its apparent cost will look about quadruple what it actually is. The cost of the belt is almost nothing—just notions and scraps you already have. To buy one similar would cost $75 on up. Don't you just love to create something terrific from nothing?

How to Make the Fancy Belt

1. Make a Stiff Belt from fabric (see page 25).

2. Twist the components loosely while arranging over the fabric belt.

3. Pin here and there to anchor temporarily. Anchor wherever necessary using a lot of little hand stitches in a blending color thread.

4. Stitch on top of this collection several beads in interesting colors and textures, as well as a combination of stone and wood, in assorted shapes and sizes.

5. Attach the ends to a two-piece buckle, the closure to be placed in center back.

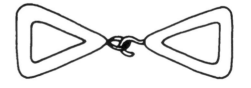

Storing Belts

When you run out of drawer space for belt storage, look to the walls or closet doors. Closet shops, container shops, and hardware stores will have a wealth of ideas to expand the storage possibilities. These may run the gamut from clear plastic boxes to decorative baskets.

Other ready-made conveniences include racks or wall holders similar to what works for hanging men's neckties, and expandable racks for hanging coffee mugs.

Dimensional Embellishments

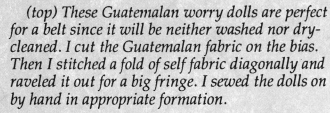

(top) These Guatemalan worry dolls are perfect for a belt since it will be neither washed nor dry-cleaned. I cut the Guatemalan fabric on the bias. Then I stitched a fold of self fabric diagonally and raveled it out for a big fringe. I sewed the dolls on by hand in appropriate formation.

(bottom) A pansy print lining prompted three-dimensional repeats on the outside. I sewed the irregularly cut suede circles on at the centers, pinching a fold in the process to give depth. Some yarn and suede foliage completed the composition.

(left) While baking one day, I noticed how a jar of stick cinnamon looked like rolled-up pieces of faux suede. Anything can inspire a belt!

(right) If you can't stitch it, glue it. Here I glued an agate slice to the suede base, with a few crushed strips partially covering it to help hold the agate in place.

It's Your Turn

This book gives several dozen ideas for starters. Now it's time for you to take off on your own. Once you start thinking creatively, the possibilities for making interesting, attractive belts are endless. All of nature and anything manmade can be the inspiration and the raw materials from which fashions spring.

If wearing belts is not your favorite thing but you like this creative process, carry out your decorative ideas on a bag instead of a belt. Small projects are the ideal place to activate the artist within you, pulling together something wearable from bits and pieces of magic.

I'd love to see what you've done. Send nonreturnable snapshots to:

Shirley Adams
PO Box 688
Plainfield, IN 46168

Index